I0006685

CYBER WARRIORS AT WAR

U.S. National Security Secrets & Fears Revealed

Dr. Berg P. Hyacinthe, PhD[*]

CYBER WARRIORS AT WAR

U.S. National Security Secrets & Fears Revealed

[*] PhD, Florida State University; Doctor of Laws (LLD Class of 2010), Sorbonne's Assas School of Law (CERSA-CNRS); Special thanks go to www.infosensing.com of Florida.

Copyright © 2009 by Dr. Berg P. Hyacinthe, PhD.

ISBN: Hardcover   978-1-4415-8170-9
          Softcover   978-1-4415-8169-3

All rights reserved. No part of this book may be reproduced or transmitted in any form or by any means, electronic or mechanical, including photocopying, recording, or by any information storage and retrieval system, without permission in writing from the copyright owner.

This book was printed in the United States of America.

To order additional copies of this book, contact:
Xlibris Corporation
1-888-795-4274
www.Xlibris.com
Orders@Xlibris.com
69210

TABLE OF CONTENTS

IN MEMORY OF

The late Sen. Edward "Teddy" Kennedy

Uncle Constantine Hyacinthe
Fallen U.S. soldiers in Iraq & Afghanistan
The 9/11 victims

Innocent Iraqi and Afghan victims

Papa "Colas" & Papa "Dukens"

Grandma "Ida"

R.I.P

FOREWORD

The Department of Defense Office of General
Counsel issued guidelines warning that
misuse of information attacks could subject
U.S. authorities to war crimes charges.
— Lt. Col. Bryan W. Ellis, U.S. Army

The United States' national security
"secret" is the fruit of (1) a lengthy
acquaintance with the rule of law and (2)
an unwavering commitment to advanced science
and technology — via the "inventiveness"
of individual citizens. Today, information
warfare (IW) plays a quintessential role in
strategic defense and security. Accordingly,
for purposes of this Essay, "IW" refers to
the adoption of information technologies as
cognitive and/or physical weapons to engage
in warfare — defined so as not to be limited
to armed conflicts — in all theaters. The
term "IW" also encompasses terrestrial,
cyberspace, and interstellar activities.

According to Lolita Baldor (quoting Lt. Gen. William Shelton, chief of the U.S. Air Force's warfighting integration unit), the military's new cyber command at Fort Meade, Maryland will be a sub-unit of U.S. Strategic Command, designed to "defend vital networks and project power in cyberspace." However, as the author has argued for many years, IW's intrinsic legal lacuna, once perceived as a strategic "advantage" to maintain information superiority and dominance, has become America's most underestimated weakness: a hidden threat to its national security and to international peace.

Space and outer space capabilities play an important role in the development, deployment, and maintenance of communications satellites and spy "spacecrafts" that feed the IW machinery. Of course, the absence of space sovereignty, an adjacent element of great concern, will continue to challenge the influence of the traditional superpowers. As Iran, North Korea, India, Japan, and other undeclared nations look "spaceward," suddenly America finds itself in a very subtle process of redefinition and reinvention. In essence, the growing number of space power contenders cannot be ignored.

The potential of terrorists and other enemies using Internet and/or other digital information technologies as transport vehicles for WMD is becoming more evident. For example, the Internet has emerged as an undeniable asymmetric — cheap and powerful — recruitment tool for terrorist organizations. The Internet is also used by extremists on both sides of the so-called war on terror as a persuasive apparatus to launch indiscriminate "cyber jihad." Simply stated, in many instances religion had been carelessly misused for personal and/or political reasons.

Separately, infightings between established superpowers have mutated from Cold War to Code War, involving "hacking" into defense and other protected computer information networks — thereby threatening critical infrastructures. For instance, built on and remotely guided by "codes," military drones are essentially versatile "flying computers" with the devastating power to hunt and kill the enemy. They are placed in the column of new, lethal IW weapons. With respect to the cyber-WMD threat, it may also involve cyber-assisted biochemical transactions, which may be processed through olfactory information exchanges, to attack civilian and military targets anytime/anywhere.

In effect, the abovementioned developments will continue to influence this widely adopted "computers-as-weapons" paradigm (as biologically-inspired systems are being developed and remotely controlled miniature robots are being produced with capabilities to disperse lethal doses by crawling or flying). Several models of users' adoption of new technology support the author's reoccurring "technological mutation" theme.

The international intelligence community has been on notice since the late 1930's. The scale might be all that has been modified from a 1944 German design of an unmanned aerial vehicle (UAV) intended to disperse deadly airborne bioactive substances — according to U.S. intelligence accounts reported in annex. Common wisdom would dictate that the design and development of UAVs and Nano Air Vehicles (NAVs) be done in parallel with very efficient autonomous biochemical decontamination/ neutralization systems — also illustrated in annex. The potential for "misusing" cybernetics as a biochemical warfare amplifier is real. The likely adoption by non-traditional and paramilitary groups of this reality and the resulting consequences should be further investigated.

This obvious race towards computer-weapon "singularity" will intensify as the world flattens and as new knowledge continues to spread in nanoseconds through creative media and innovative channels to a *new class* of enemies: cyber-conditioned terrorists. It will require inventive, highly trained cyber warriors, working together with attentive policymakers, to overcome the challenge ahead, within the boundaries of the rule of law.

But insofar, ill-conceived efforts to distance America from its core values (e.g., its acquaintance with the rule of law) have proven to be unwise, dangerous to its strategic standing on the world stage, and in some cases, as the U.S. Supreme Court recently held in *Hamdan* v. *Rumsfeld*, downright unconstitutional. As a result, 21st century cyber warriors are often confronted with career-threatening decisions when dealing with multifarious interactions between IW weapons, armed conflicts, and the rule of law.

This Essay offers a rare look into the secret evolution of IW, from weapons of mass disruption to weapons of mass destruction (WMD) and interplanetary weapons of final solution.

The evolution of modern computer systems as weapons of war compels wary jurists to turn to the laws that should govern development and use of lethal information technologies.

Professor Louise Doswald-Beck, Director of the University Centre for International Humanitarian Law of the Geneva Graduate Institute of International Studies, has postulated that, whenever something useful for the improvement of human life has been invented, thoughts will turn to how to weaponize or destroy it, or, in the case of computer network technology, both. In this Essay, Dr. Berg P. Hyacinthe draws on his post-doctoral research, which covers the broad utilization of computers as weapons of war (e.g., in armed conflicts) to discuss the quiet fusion of digital telecommunication networks and bio-microelectromechanical systems (BIO-MEMS) into potential diffusers and transport vehicle of WMD. Dr. Hyacinthe reports from extensive research conducted toward the completion of his doctorate degree at Florida State University, where he focused on Information Warfare, Emergent Technologies, and Social Informatics.

Upon completing his PhD in 2007, Dr. Hyacinthe attempted to say goodbye to student life. However, he quickly realized — through Prof. Louise Doswald-Beck's above cited revelations, Prof. John N. Gathegi's position at the intersection of technology and the rule of law, and Prof. Gilles J. Guglielmi's brilliant juristic approach to the notions of IW conducts, IW damages, and IW responsibilities — that the establishment of a juridical notion of IW could serve as a "down payment" on long-lasting peace and security at home and abroad. In response, Dr. Hyacinthe later entered Assas School of Law at La Sorbonne, where he is currently working toward narrowing what has been perceived as a dangerous legal "black hole" in the evolution of lethal information technologies as weapons of war.

With a growing list of nations aspiring to space power, Dr. Hyacinthe treats IW's current state of "legal ambiguity" not only as a threat to the national security of the United States, but more importantly as a hidden interplanetary threat to the survival of mankind. For instance, regrettably intercontinental ballistic missile technologies are evolving into interplanetary threats of WMD. The interstellar danger is looming.

Dr. Hyacinthe is a U.S. patent holder featured in Harvard's Smithsonian/NASA

Astrophysics Data System for pioneering the patent-pending concept of autonomous neutralization of an array of airborne bioactive threats to public safety. Three of his patent applications have been published through the United States Patent and Trade Office. He often acknowledges constructive feedback received from conferences held at the U.S. Naval Postgraduate School, Monterey (as author); Defence Academy of the United Kingdom, Shrivenham (as invited session Chair); and National Defense College, Helsinki (session Chair). He is currently completing a Doctor of Laws (LLD) at La Sorbonne. Most recently, Dr. Hyacinthe served as Assistant Professor and Scientific Advisor to Taibah University's Strategic Science & Advanced Technology Unit.

His Essay introduces initial discussions on a proposed juridical notion of IW — a synergistic approach combining law and emergent digital technologies to protect cyber warriors against potential charges of having committed IW war crimes and/or IW crimes against humanity. Humanitarian concerns *vis-à-vis* IW victims are addressed accordingly. Further, to illustrate the multifaceted nature of the cyber warrior's field of intervention, the author discloses several exploitable homeland security patents and concepts — conveniently placed in annex.

To defense and intelligence officials, the author exposes several hidden global security threats associated with emergent digital information technologies and proposes potential solutions (e.g., physical cyber security, autonomous emergency response systems, bio-inspired defense/security systems). To jurists, legal analysts, policymakers, and other information professionals, he highlights domestic and international legal implications of IW involving WMD (e.g., potential violations of international laws through the use of lethal information technologies). To business executives and research scientists, he draws several sharp angles on intellectual/industrial property issues, cybercrimes, corporate espionage, and business intelligence.

Finally, to the growing population of technologically and scientifically literate generalists, students of any academic discipline, this Essay offers a fertile ground to ignite creativity, foster inventiveness, and activate the thrust for further research.

A Domestic Law Approach to the Juridical Notion of Information Warfare

Protecting cyber warriors against potential charges
of having committed IW war crimes and/or IW crimes
against humanity will require a significant level of
harmony between military instructions
and the rule of law.

I. INTRODUCTION

The success of pre-emptive strikes and decisive military operations depends profoundly upon both reliable human intelligence and the versatile skills of 21st century "cyber warriors" whose Information Operations (IO) activities are conducted through modern warfare's pentagonal synchrony — land, sea, air, cyberspace, and outer space. Technologically, Command-and-Control over these five functions is developing towards its full "interstellar" potential. Unfortunately, however, these operations are commonly effectuated under a legal regime that is ambiguous in important ways. Of course, based on previous exemplary attempts,[2] the time has now come to regulate IW. But how, and under what legal framework? Cognizant of the need to establish explicit IW guidelines for the protection of cyber warriors and potential IW victims alike, the author will argue in favor of a domestic law approach to IW.

This Essay proposes a foundational domestic law approach to IW, with the primary objective of overcoming the widely-documented shortcomings of international law in the complex realm of 21st century warfare. It is worth noting that illustrations of the proposed "domestic paradigm" will rely primarily on U.S.-related examples and analogies. (For purposes of this Essay, "IW" refers to the adoption of information technologies as cognitive and/or physical weapons to engage in warfare — defined so as not to be limited to armed conflicts — in all theaters. The term "IW" also encompasses terrestrial, cyberspace, and interstellar activities).

Granted, domestic law precedents related to IW remain rare, but this area of law is growing at a phenomenal speed. Many cases in the area of corporate computer crime have already been recorded.[3] Other instances involve the use of lethal IW weapons in armed conflicts (e.g., in Afghanistan, Eastern Europe, Iraq, Pakistan, Palestine, Yemen, and elsewhere) and network attacks against critical infrastructures (e.g., the Ehud Tenenbaum case, the Gary McKinnon case, Estonia's "cyber bombardment" case, and various alleged intrusions into the U.S. Defense systems by foreign spies).[4] The

U.S. military is well aware of the danger
ahead. For instance, David J. Dicenso,
Associate Professor of Law at the United
States Air Force Academy, described the
following hypothetical scenario on July 31,
2000:

> [An Iraqi national] learned all that
> he could about computers, networks,
> computer telecommunications protocols, and
> system architecture at U.S. educational
> institutions. Now he's a graduate, at home in
> Iraq. He's been hired by a foreign terrorist
> group to infiltrate U.S. Department of Defense
> (DoD) computers to gather intelligence on
> U.S. military operations . . . Suddenly,
> the U.N. forces in Bosnia received beans
> instead of bullets. The personnel records
> of all deployed U.S. forces suddenly
> disappeared. Instead of receiving expected
> e-mail traffic, in-theater leaders received
> strings of computer-generated obscenities
> and irrelevant passages from the World Book
> Encyclopedia.[5]

Currently, the law of IW fails to answer a
series of important questions: When do cyber
warriors commit war crimes? How can the law
take into account humanitarian concerns? What

about possible constitutional encroachments? To further complicate matters, the perpetual nature of certain IW activities makes it difficult to determine when war begins and ends (a question paralleling the concern about a potentially perpetual "war on terror"). Congress makes no declarations of perpetual IW involving armed conflicts. Thus, Maj. Richard W. Aldrich of the U.S. Air Force was forced to ask, "How do you know you are at war in the Information Age?"[6] Similarly, Cmdr. James N. Bond, JAGC, U.S. Navy, questioned the legality of "peacetime foreign data manipulation as one aspect of offensive information warfare."[7] Moreover, the most disturbing and worrying questions of all come from a cadre of humanitarian legal scholars and concern the potential for the quiet mutation of IW weapons of mass disruption into physical weapons of mass destruction (PWMD), a technology-enhanced, interplanetary threat. According to the U.S. Congress, "In January 2007, China successfully tested a direct-ascent ASAT missile against a Chinese weather satellite, demonstrating its ability to attack satellites operating in low-Earth orbit. The direct ascent ASAT system is one component of a multi-dimensional program to generate the capability to deny others access to outer space."[8] As this evidence demonstrates, the interstellar threat is very real: alluring to undeniable weapons of final solution. How and why do these weapon systems threaten the survival of mankind?

In early 2008, European scientists detected the first confirmed Earthlike planet outside our solar system: the CoRoT-7b — named after the 30-centimeter space telescope (CoRoT), launched by the European Space Agency in December 2006. CoRoT's primary objective ("Detect Rocky Planets Outside the Solar System,") combined with the findings reported during the Barcelona conference ("Pathways Towards Habitable Planets") that followed in October 2009, did not leave any doubt with regard to a not-too-secret ambition: assuring the survival of *Homo Sapiens* beyond Earth's capillary boundaries.

Now, if the threat is state-based, domestic statutes or international remedies should be able to regulate it. If the threat emanates from non-state actors, their home or resident countries should be able to take criminal action against them.

In Section I, the author examines how certain military operations within IW require a new legal framework, and recounts specific events involving various forms of IW conduct and cyber attack. Section II compares domestic and international approaches. Section III looks at specific cases of domestic, international, and interstellar legal implications of IW; it also provides a synopsis of each approach, followed by a review of existing laws that bind the U.S. Section IV covers policy implications pertaining to the notion of separation of powers that is deeply anchored in the U.S. Constitution and found in the judicial systems of most contemporary democracies. Section V discusses some limitations and imperfections of the proposed domestic law approach, and highlights areas for further research. Section VI carries out an extrapolation on some of the author's prior foresight analyses. Lastly, Section VII concludes with a context-driven deconstruction of several key elements of Barack Obama's national security agendum, and highlights the challenges ahead. In annex, the author provides graphical illustrations of the multifaceted nature of his area of intervention.

ENDNOTES-I

*   PhD, Florida State University; Doctor of Laws
     (LLD Class of 2010), Sorbonne's Assas School
     of Law (CERSA-CNRS); Special thanks go to www.
     infosensing.com of Florida.

2   Sean P. Kanuck, Note, *Information Warfare:
     New Challenges for Public International
     Law*, HARV. INT'L L.J. 37 272-289 (1996); Eric
     Tablot Jensen, *Computer Attacks on Critical
     National Infrastructure: A Use of Force
     Invoking the Right of Self-Defense*, 38 STAN.
     J. INT'L L. 207 (2002); LAWRENCE T. GREENBERG,
     SEYMOUR E. GOODMAN, & KEVIN HOO, INFORMATION WARFARE
     AND INTERNATIONAL LAW (1999); Christopher Joyner
     & Catherine Lotrionte, *Information Warfare as
     International Coercion: Elements of a Legal
     Framework*, 12 EUR. J. INT'L L. 825, 825-865
     (2001); Thomas Wingfield, *Legal Aspects of
     Offensive Information Operations in Space*, 9
     J. LEGAL STUD. (U.S. Air Force Academy) 9, 121
     (1999); JAMES BOND, PEACETIME FOREIGN DATA MANIPULATION
     AS ONE ASPECT OF OFFENSIVE INFORMATION WARFARE: QUESTIONS
     OF LEGALITY UNDER THE UNITED NATIONS CHARTER ARTICLE
     2(4) (1996), *available at* http://handle.
     dtic.mil/100.2/ADA310926 (last visited Dec.
     11, 2008) (discussing whether manipulation

of a foreign state's data may be considered
to be the use of force against that country
in violation of Article 2(4) of the U.N.
Charter, and reviewing different methods
of interpreting treaties such as the U.N.
Charter); Michael J. Robbat, *Resolving the
Legal Issues Concerning the Use of Information
Warfare in the International Forum: The
Reach of the Existing Legal Framework and
the Creation of a New Paradigm*, 6 B.U. J.
SCI. & TECH. L. 10 (2000); David J. DiCenso,
*IW Cyberlaw: The Legal Issues of Information
Warfare*, AIRPOWER J. 13, 85 (1999); STANLEY S.
ARKIN *ET AL.*, PREVENTION AND PROSECUTION OF COMPUTER AND
HIGH TECHNOLOGY CRIME (1989); Michael N. Schmitt,
Thomas Wingfield, & Heather Harrison-Dinniss,
Computers and War: The Legal Battlespace,
HUMANITARIAN POLICY AND CONFLICT RESEARCH AT HARVARD
UNIVERSITY, (June 24, 2004), *available at* http://
www.ihlresearch.org/ihl/pdfs/schmittetal.pdf
(last visited Feb. 12, 2009); Bryan W. Ellis,
*The International Legal Implications and
Limitations of Information Warfare: What Are
Our Options?*, *available at* http://www.iwar.
org.uk/law/resources/iwlaw/Ellis_B_W_01.pdf
(last visited Aug. 28, 2008); Davis Brown,
Proposal for an International Convention to

Regulate the Use of Information Systems in Armed Conflict, 47 Harv. Int'l L.J. 179 (2006) (discussing IW in both corporate (civilian) and military settings).

3   *See* M. Zuckerman, *Security on Trial in Case of On-line Citibank Heist*, USA Today, Sept. 19, at 12A (1997); Peter A. Lupsha, *Transnational Organized Crime Versus the Nation State*, 2 Transnat'l Organized Crime 21, 34 (1996); David J. Loundy, Computer Crime, Information Warfare, and Economic Espionage (2003).

4   For discussion of armed conflicts, *see* Schmitt *et al.*, *supra* note 2, at 1 (note 2) (reporting CIA use of remotely-controlled Predator to attack a car carrying an alleged Al Qaida senior operative in Yemen, Qaed Senyan al Harthi); *see also* Scott Lindlaw, *Remote-control Warriors Suffer War Stress*, Associated Press, (Aug. 7, 2008), *available at* http://www.msnbc.msn.com/id/26078087 (last visited Nov. 29, 2008) (describing stressful state of cyber warriors operating 7,000 miles away from Southern California dropping 500-pound bombs at the speed of 500-600 mph). Moreover, according to Voice of America News (VOA), "[T]here have been more than 30 missile strikes targeting alleged militants in Pakistan since

August. They are believed to have been carried out by U.S. remote-controlled aircraft[s]. U.S. authorities have refused to confirm or deny responsibility for the attacks." *See Suspected US Missile Strike in Pakistan Kills 6,* (VOA News, Dec. 11, 2008), *available at* http://www.voanews.com/english/2008-12-11-voa47.cfm?textmode=0 (last visited Dec. 16, 2008); BBC News reported earlier (e.g., as of Nov. 7, 2008) that "[T]here are believed to have been 18 strikes by CIA-operated predator drones in Pakistan's tribal border areas since August." *See 'US strike' on Pakistan militants,* BBC NEWS (Nov. 7, 2008), *available at* http://news.bbc.co.uk/2/hi/south_asia/7714844.stm (last visited Jan. 20, 2009). In summary, similar to activities reported during the brief Russian-Georgia conflict in the Caucasus in 2008, "killer drone" activities continue to be very frequent along the Pakistan-Afghan border. On the other side of the spectrum, improvised explosive devices (IEDs) have become the trademark of insurgents in Iraq and elsewhere. Did James Adams's "NEXT WORLD WAR (1998)" come sooner than expected?

The Ehud Tenenbaum case involved an Israeli teenager (the "Analyzer") arrested on

suspicion of hacking his way into Pentagon
and other sensitive computer systems.
Tenenbaum reportedly tapped into as many as
700 sites worldwide; among other sites, he
allegedly broke into computers belonging to
President Ezer Weizman, the Israeli Knesset,
and Palestinian extremist organizations.
Other U.S. targets included NASA, several U.S.
Air Force and Navy systems, many U.S.
universities and federally-funded research
sites such as the Lawrence Livermore National
Laboratory. *See* Rebecca Trounson, *Hacker Case
Taps Into Fame, Fury,* LA Times, Apr. 27, at
A-1 (1998).

Gary McKinnon, known as "Solo," is a British
hacker who has claimed to be a UFO investigator
in response to charges of perpetrating the
"biggest military computer hack of all time"
against U.S. military information systems.
He reportedly broke into more than 73,000 US
government computers, including those of the
US Army, Navy, and NASA, and deleted critical
data. He was arrested in 2002 by British police
and faced extradition to the U.S. Similarly,
see Bob Drogin, *Yearlong Hacker Attack Nets
Sensitive U.S. Data,* L.A. TIMES, Oct. 7, at A1
(1999) (reporting on constant attacks against

U.S. Defense systems by foreign spies).
Interestingly, "analyzer" and "solo" have not
been classified as spies, though Analyzer's
case is still pending before U.S. courts.

 Lastly, by many accounts, Estonia has been
considered to be the site of the first State-
sponsored cyber attack, although Gulf War
I against the Saddam regime involved many
State-sponsored IO activities: the Estonian
case involved a three-week wave of massive
"cyber-attacks" on the tiny Baltic state. *See
The Cyber Raiders Hitting Estonia*, BBC News
(May 17, 2007), *available at* http://news.bbc.
co.uk/2/hi/europe/6665195.stm (last visited
Nov. 22, 2008)(indirectly implicating Russian
cyber warriors).

[5]   David J. DiCenso, *Information Operations: An
Act of War?*, Air & Space Power Journal, (Maxwell
Air Force Base, Jul. 31, 2000), *available
at* http://www.airpower.maxwell.af.mil/
airchronicles/cc/DiCenso1.html (last visited
March 2, 2009).

[6]   Richard W. Aldrich, *How Do You Know You
Are at War in the Information Age?* 22 Hous.
J. Int'l L. 223 (2000); *see also* Columbia
Law Review. Editors, *Legal Aspects of
Reconnaissance in Airspace and Outer Space*,

61 Colum. L. Rev. 1074 (1961) (suggesting that
reconnaissance [in airspace and outer space]
should be held to violate international
law only if its means were to involve an
independent breach thereof). Accordingly,
for the purpose of this Essay, cyberspace
is submitted under the same investigative
lenses. For supportive arguments, *see* Spenser
M. Beresford, *Surveillance Aircraft and
Satellites: A Problem of International Law*,
27 J. Air L. & Commerce, 107, 107 (1960)
(confirming Beresford's prescient legal
concerns, pertaining to what are referred
to today as the interstellar implications of
IW). Beresford went on to serve as general
counsel for NASA between 1963 and 1973.

7   *See* BOND, *supra* note 2; *see also* Duncan B.
Hollis, *Why States Need an International Law
for Information Operations*, 11 LEWIS & CLARK L.
REV. 1023 (2007); *see also* MARC B. TREADWELL, WHEN
DOES AN ACT OF INFORMATION WARFARE BECOME AN ACT OF WAR?
AMBIGUITY IN PERCEPTION (1998), (Carlisle Barracks
Army War College, May 17, 1998), *available at*
http://handle.dtic.mil/100.2/ada345572 (last
visited Nov. 22, 2008) (addressing similar
issues confronted by Col. James Bond and Maj.
Richard Aldrich).

8   US Department of Defense, Annual Report to Congress: Military Power of the People's Republic of China 2007, at 20-23 (2007), *available at* http://www.fas. org/ nuke/ guide/ china/ dod- 2007.pdf (last visited May 18, 2008)(capturing Col. Yuan Zelu's ambition: [T]he goal of a space shock and awe strike is [to] deter the enemy, not to provoke the enemy into combat. For this reason, the objectives selected for strike must be few and precise . . . [for example] on important information sources, command and control centers, communications hubs, and other objectives. This will shake the structure of the opponent's operational system of organization and will create huge psychological impact on the opponent's policymakers).

See also Treaties and Principles on Space Law, (United Nations), *available at* http://www. oosa.unvienna.org/oosa/SpaceLaw/treaties. html (last visited March 19, 2009) (outlining five international legal instruments and five sets of legal principles governing space-related activities: Outer Space Treaty of 1967 (governing the activities of Member States in the exploration and use of outer space, including the Moon and other celestial bodies);

The Rescue Agreement of 1968 (covering the rescue and return of astronauts as well as the return of objects launched into outer space); The Liability Convention of 1972 (establishing international liability for damage caused by space objects); The Registration Convention of 1975 (requiring the registration of objects launched into outer space); The Moon Agreement of 1979 (governing the activities of Member States on the Moon and other celestial bodies)).

Though these "agreements" seem to cover certain aspects of the interstellar dimension of IW, they were apparently signed under the premises that space and outer space would remain the "province of mankind," restricted to "peaceful purposes," and "free of any weapons." Currently, Member States face a new reality. Engaging (legally) in hostilities "through" outer space seems to require a new paradigm: new rules of engagement for cyber warriors. *See* Richard Allen Greene, *First Rocky Planet Found Outside* Solar System, (CNN NEWS, October 7, 2009), *available at* http://edition.cnn.com/2009/TECH/space/09/16/new.rocky.planet/index.html (last visited October 7, 2009) (describing an Earthlike planet and

contrasting it with gaseous ones like Jupiter
and Saturn, while likening it to Mercury and
Venus — confirming a not-closely-held secret
ambition to assure interstellar living).

II. IW's Domestic/ International Law Dichotomy

To date, previous IW regulatory attempts appear to have been linked to a very popular — but nonetheless premature — international law approach. In many instances, however, regulators have concluded that this approach does not apply to most IO activities.[9] Thus, the author will argue that the present juridical notion of IW must be expanded to establish the legal framework necessary to undertake the issues surrounding IO. Toward this end, it is important to focus upon three key concepts: (1) IW conduct, (2) IW damages, and (3) IW responsibilities.

"IW conduct" refers to real or virtual IW activities, using information technologies as weapons, which arises either out of legitimate necessity (for instance, corporate self-defense or military necessity) or out of misconduct or crime.[10] For example, if a country's military were to use surveillance aircraft in coordination or synchronization with communications satellites and military drones, then that would be considered a sequence of IW conduct. Criminal IW conducts may involve spreading virus via Internet[11] or knowingly using lethal IW weapons against innocent civilians during armed conflicts and in other contexts.

In international law, a new form of conduct is accepted as a "crime" only following an exhaustive analysis of the context in which it occurs.[12] In domestic law, however, once particular conduct is defined as a crime by statute, a full consideration of context and the invocation of discretionary measures do not occur until the sentencing phase — and even then, mandatory sentencing guidelines may constrain judges' discretion. In the U.S., for example, mandatory sentencing guidelines remain a very thorny issue. Recently, the Supreme Court held in *United States v. Booker* and *United States v. Fanfan* that federal judges are no longer bound by the U.S. Sentencing Guidelines, but need only consult them when they punish federal criminals. Still, failure to consult the Guidelines may trigger arguments in favor of vacating a judge's decision.

Sentencing guidelines also are employed in other countries. In France, a new Penal Code — which entered into force in 1994 — updated the previous Penal Code of 1810, which had set most of the rules on sentencing. For example, Art. 111(1) of the new Penal Code specifies a tripartite division of offenses based on their seriousness, and sets out the range of penalties for each type of offense. In the United Kingdom, the Sentencing Advisory Panel was established under the Crime and Disorder Act of 1998, the purpose of which was to promote consistency in sentencing. The Criminal Justice Act of 2003 subsequently established a Sentencing Guidelines Council charged with issuing such guidelines. Germany's Code of Criminal Procedure, which is part of its Penal Code, sets out the general provisions for sentencing, with the broad range of authorized sentences for each offense-type set out in several sections of the code. A minimum fixed term of one month of imprisonment is set forth in paragraph 38, while paragraph 47 offers "conditional" probation as an alternative to mandatory imprisonment of less than six months.

The term "IW damages" encompasses all the negative results of IW techniques, methods and weapons: from physical destruction, to quantifiable devaluation/depreciation of assets,[13] to other losses, to psychological traumas, including the results of torture. For example, this definition would include traceable sensory damages stemming from the misuse of digital imageries and of sounds. Certain spectral weapons may cause serious injuries, physical destruction, and quantifiable devaluation of assets.[14]

"IW responsibilities" are the duties imposed on those who use IW conduct unlawfully, in such a way as to cause damages to persons or property. Such responsibilities are typically enforced by a civil or criminal action against the aggressor.[15] Damages must be concrete and real: If a commercial communications satellite collides with a military spacecraft, damages from debris would count, but not claims of "harms from being spied on." Simply put, there must be real harms to real victims.

Historically, intent and prior knowledge are necessary if a violation is to be proven; domestic laws typically require the offense be performed "knowingly" and "willfully." In the case of IW, the level of training and technological expertise required to build and effectively deliver sophisticated IW weapon

systems will likely shatter the common line
of defense "I was simply following orders."
Accordingly, the general perception of cyber
warriors as the "smartest kids on the block"
may make convictions more likely.

What about international regulation of
IW? Professor Davis Brown, former Deputy
Staff Judge Advocate at the U.S. Defense
Information Systems Agency, went back to
"the basic principles of military necessity,
proportionality, humanity, chivalry, and
distinction" to propose international
regulations for the use of information systems
in armed conflict. However, although these
principles are very broad in nature and
written in plain language, they fail to cover
certain aspects of IW. In addition, thorny
venue and jurisdiction issues arise for, as
Professor Brown pointed out, "Cyberspace is
nowhere."[16]

Venue, jurisdiction, and enforceability
issues may be less troubling, however, with
respect to a domestic law approach such as
the one this Essay advocates.[17] IW conduct,
IW damage, and IW responsibility can be
determined as a matter of fact — through
digital forensics, aerial surveillance,
and advanced scientific damage assessment

methods/tools. There are real human victims and quantifiable physical damages; their identity may be used to determine if there is a sufficient connection to a particular jurisdiction. The more concrete definitions of domestic law may be more helpful, in this respect, than the potentially vague and ambiguous terms of international conventions and treaties. As Col. Bryan Ellis has noted, "a nation's domestic criminal law directly affects the assistance that the nation can provide in suppressing certain behavior by persons operating in its territory." [18] Indeed, "a nation's domestic law may limit U.S. information operations conducted in the nation's territory or involving communications routed through the nation's communications systems."[19]

Hence, the author will argue that the domestic law approach promises a more pragmatic, efficient pathway to regulation,[20] — one that may include both constitutional limits and concrete enforceability. (Ultimately, such an approach may also influence a later international regime, for treaties and conventions are often based on Member States' domestic legal regimes). The domestic law approach has its weaknesses: it may allow for "convenient" or politically-biased interpretations of law by domestic judges.[21] Yet the author will argue that it is still a superior approach because it provides checks and balances, and may take advantage of a large historical *corpus* of prior precedents on which to ground interpretation (*see* Table I below).[22]

TABLE I. DOMESTIC V. INTERNATIONAL JURISTIC APPROACHES

Strength: Domestic Law Approach	Weakness: International Law Approach
Enforceable	Often unenforceable
Reliance on legal tenets backed by enforcement mechanisms and/or a constitution	Reliance on Member States' "voluntary" agreements
Long-standing precedent to draw upon	Less than a century of "real" jurisprudence
Strong checks and balances	"Watchdog" role
Basic tenets: conduct, damage, responsibility, specifically defined by statute	Normative instruments (e.g., treaty, accord, and convention) may lack sufficiently specific definition of terms

Remarkably, in certain circumstances where espionage and military intelligence are involved,[23] the responsible parties are often impossible to identify beyond a

reasonable doubt or according to the rule
of law — despite the fact that there has
been undeniable misconduct, causing actual
damages.

In the end, legislation may prove more
promising than case law precedent here.
Around the world, countries and localities
are enacting legislation in the areas
of cybercrime, cyber terrorism, digital
information privacy, and Internet security.
There has been progress on these fronts at the
international level as well.[24] However, due to
the "digital divide" between those who do and
do not possess effective access to vital 21st
century information technologies, few nations
possess both the required scientific and legal
expertise to tackle some of the deadliest IW
threats discussed in this Essay. In fact,
according to a comprehensive review of a series
of U.N. General Assembly resolutions covering
about a decade (from UNGA 53/70 of December
4, 1998 to UNGA 62/17 of January 8, 2008) on
the subject, many Member States appear to be
unaware of the gravity of the problems they
currently face (see Appendices).

In crafting domestic law solutions, other
valuable resources also exist — including
academic theses, military memoirs, articles and

books — to suggest the types of legislations that lawmakers should formulate.[25] As such, the goal would be to focus upon IW conduct, damage, and responsibility, and rely upon doctrine, jurisprudence, legislation, and other resources, such as these, to produce new rules, based on universally accepted cardinal principles, that will be more effective than international treaties for the moment.

An important aspect of such rules is a doctrine of "checks and balances" such as that found, for example, in the U.S. Constitution's separation of powers.[26] The importance of separation of powers in the U.S. was demonstrated by Professors Neal Katyal and Laurence Tribe's defiant warning to the Bush Administration in 2002 that the executive could not simply override Congress and the judiciary when it came to the treatment of detainees: "Ours is 'a government of laws and not of men.'"[27] Professor Katyal went on to lead the team of lawyers that prevailed in restoring rights to Guantanamo detainees in *Hamdan v. Rumsfeld*.[28]

In 1958, through Common Law of Mankind, Jenks proposed a "fusion" of various legal traditions, but heterogeneous judicial traditions nonetheless persisted.[29] Today's general consensus, in international law, tends to reject Jenks's "fusion" approach, and lean toward deferring to the "cultural diversity" approach instead — an approach inspired, in part, by Grotius's voluntarism.[30] As emergent powerful States continue to challenge traditional superpowers and remap the geopolitical landscape to reflect new realities,[31] voluntarism is likely to continue to dominate.

Unfortunately, across Member States' domestic legal regimes, law in the area of IW remains undeveloped. Such domestic law would be valuable not only in itself, but also as a model for possible future international solutions. (Though the Geneva Convention may provide strong analogies here, it will not solve the fundamental problem). Legal scholars would need a tested model (ideally, the very first explicit domestic IW statute), before aspiring to devise an ideal international treaty regime for IW. By comparison, without an explicit domestic statute to serve as a model, there was unprecedented delay in the international community's reaching an agreement on the Biological Warfare Convention of 1972.[32] Member States should be wary of repeating that delay when it comes to IW, and allowing a partial legal vacuum in this area to persist.

In suggesting domestic legal frameworks, the legal framework that French scholar Jean Deglaire established in the aftermath of World War I may prove helpful. Deglaire established "certainty" (*dommage à caractère certain*) and "material" (*dommage à caractère réel*) as two cardinal requirements for the legal classification of war damages, and also emphasized universal legal pillars such as responsibility and damage.[33] As Deglaire's work suggests, setting forth material facts as to responsibility and damage should be at the core of any proposed domestic IW solution — despite the difficulty of establishing such facts in cyberspace. Professor Louise Doswald-Beck of the *Institut des Hautes Études Internationales de Genève* has postulated that whenever something useful for the improvement of human life has been invented, thoughts will turn to how to weaponize or destroy it, or, in the case of computer network technology, both.[34] Indeed, digital information technologies have already been lethally weaponized. Cyberspace allows for worldwide and interplanetary reach (e.g., via space satellites and other activities affecting celestial bodies), thus increasing geometrically the potential threat of WMD.

IW devices and techniques — physical, psychological, and virtual[35] — that cause "material damage" to real individuals and critical infrastructures are, in effect, IW weapons that can and should be regulated. The daunting task of identifying the culprits does not justify the continuous effort to maintain the dangerously dysfunctional IW *status quo*. The U.S. Air Force, considered the lead agency for IW within the U.S. Department of Defense, defines weapons as "devices" designed to kill, injure, or disable people, and do damage or destroy property, but sent a mixed signal in 1994 via the clause "weapons do not include . . . electronic warfare devices."[36] Ultimately, U.S. Air Force legal scholars took a closer look at the issue, and treated it more cautiously thereafter.[37]

Several years and many technology cycles later, today's electronic warfare devices have emerged as real and very lethal weapons. In fact, many computer technologies (currently embedded, fused, or mutated with very lethal weapons), involved in major IO activities, are designed to kill, injure, or disable people, and do damage or destroy property.

Professor Michael N. Schmitt — who has
recently held the positions of Charles H.
Stockton Visiting Chair of International Law
at the United States Naval War College, Sir
Ninian Stephen Visiting Scholar at Melbourne
University, and Visiting Scholar at Yale
Law School — made the following remark with
regard to computers and wars: ". . . we have
witnessed their transformation into a 'means
of warfare' (weapon) and modern militaries
are busily developing information technology
methods of warfare."[38]

Even after accounting for notable contextual
differences, the general consensus is that
the definition of "weapon" should depend not
only on its physical aspect, but also — and
largely — on its intended use.[39] Hence, this
"intended use" principle presents a very
credible challenge to any interpretation
or misinterpretation of the U.S. Air Force
directive (AFPD-51-4) as a basis to claim
that electronic warfare devices that kill,
injure, or disable people, do damage, or
destroy property are nevertheless not weapons.
Unfortunately, the existing anarchical IW
paradigm involves an array of unspecified
and unmonitored electronic devices that
kill, injure, or disable people, do damage or

destroy property.[40] In other words, the current situation is full of devices that urgently need to be legally recognized as what, in fact, they function as: weapons.

Such recognition would be supported by authoritative arguments from U.S. military experts and a significant number of international jurists.[41] According to the literature, IO activities are commonly conducted under the umbrella of an evolving IW doctrine, which calls for information dominance and/or total paralysis, via sophisticated information attacks, of an "enemy's ability" to respond. Simply put, such IO activities account for military actions taken against adversarial information systems prior to, during, or after an attack. These "adversarial information systems" unfortunately involve social networks that, historically, have been protected under military rules of armed conflict of the "civilized world" and further shielded against war crimes via the Geneva Conventions[42] and the Additional Protocols: the humanitarian concerns are, therefore, self-evident.

Furthermore, given that many military systems make use of civilian information infrastructures, IO planners must walk a fine line between serving military objectives and remaining attentive to humanitarian concerns. According to credible U.S. intelligence sources, a significant percentage of U.S. military and intelligence community voice and data communications is carried over facilities owned by public carriers.[43] In many parts of the world, similarly, civilian information infrastructures are highly connected to military and/or government-managed information systems. Of course, it will take longer for less-developed countries to conduct military operations solely on/against legitimate military targets.[44] Therefore, it is imperative that IW planners vigilantly account for socio-cultural cues before launching full-scale IO, which may hinder access to "vital information connections."[45] Otherwise, the resulting denial of basic humanitarian and emergency rescue services to non-combatants could further complicate the issue at hand.

Though weapons used in IO may be less tangible than bullets and swords, the potential victims are subject to as much (if not more) pain, suffering, and humiliation.[46] Thus, it is appropriate that humanitarian concerns and universally accepted standards of human dignity set scope and limits for such operations, even in the absence of explicit international prohibitions of IW weapons.[47] As mentioned earlier, according to Col. Ellis, "[C]urrent U.S. criminal statutes apply to Information operations. Similarly, foreign criminal statutes will most likely apply to U.S. information activities."[48] He added that "Misuse of information attacks could subject U.S. authorities to war crimes [prosecutions]."[49]

The establishment of a timely, equitable balance between military necessity and humanitarian concerns in this context thus requires a strong, enforceable IW legal regime. As the author has noted above, a domestic law approach is more likely both to be an enforceable approach, and to offer a large, coherent set of precedents on which to draw.[50]

ENDNOTES-II

9   *See* Ellis, *supra* note 2; DiCenso, *supra* note
     2; *see also* Emily Haslam, *Information Warfare:*
     Technological Changes and International Law,
     5 J. CONFLICT & SEC. L. 2 (2000); Michael N.
     Schmitt, *War, Technology, and International*
     Humanitarian Law, HPCR INT'L, (Occasional
     paper#4, Summer 2005), *available at* http://
     www.hpcr.org/pdfs/OccasionalPaper4.pdf
     (last visited Feb. 14, 2009); Wingfield,
     supra note 2.

10   *See* Neal Kumar Katyal, *Architecture as*
     Crime Control, 111 YALE L.J. 1039, 1039
     (2002) (linking the regulation of behavior
     in cyberspace to the regulation of behavior
     in real space); *see also* Neal Kumar Katyal,
     Digital Architecture as Crime Control, 112
     Yale L.J. 2261 (2003) (using the principles
     of real space architecture — opportunities
     for surveillance, territoriality, community
     building, and protection of targets — to deal
     with security/insecurity in cyberspace).

11   *See* 18 U.S.C. §§ 1030(a)(5)(A)(1994)(making
     "conduct" which intended to damage a protected
     computer a crime); Patrick J. Leahy, *New Laws*
     for New Technologies: Current Issues Facing
     the Subcommittee on Technology and the Law,

5 Harv. J. L. & Tech. 1, 21 (1992) (debating on new laws concerning the protection of people who transmit a virus through seemingly legal means); Dorothy E. Denning, INFORMATION WARFARE AND SECURITY 214 (1999) (referring to malicious code executed via a buffer overflow as executing with the privileges of the program it exploits, which is often root); *see also* Lawrence Lessig, *The Path of Cyberlaw*, 104 Yale L.J. 1743, 1746 (1995).

12   *See* Bond, *supra* note 2, at 31-33 (discussing textual, contextual, and suggestive interpretations).

13   C.F.R. § 121.1 XIII (b)(1)(1996) (listing "cryptographic (including key management) systems" and other software materials as defense articles, while exempting decryption systems for the protection of the banking system against potential IW damages); *see also* Brown, *supra* note 2, at 180 (acknowledging that "computer technology has advanced to the point where military forces now have the capability to inflict injury, death, and destruction via cyberspace."

14   U.S. Patent U.S. 6,377,436 B1 (disclosing powerful laser applications likely to increase the lethality of an array of IW weapons).

These IW weapons can cause severe damages to critical infrastructures.

15 Leahy, supra *note* 11, at 21 (seeking to hold cyber criminals accountable through new laws for new technologies).

16 *See* Brown, *supra* note 2, at 180 (commenting on cyberspace as a medium of warfare). In so doing, Brown illustrates the normative nature of *international instruments* — historically too weak and/or not explicit enough to challenge the anarchic state of IW weapons and techniques. For similar international approaches, *see* Ruth G. Wedgwood, *Proportionality, Cyberwar, and the Law of War*, 76 Int'l. L. Stud. 219, 222 (2002); Richard W. Aldrich, *The International Legal Implications of Information Warfare*, 10 AIRPOWER J. 99, 99-110 (1996) (establishing IW as broad enough to embrace concepts as old as war and as new as the latest technology); Michael N. Schmitt, *Precision Attack and International Humanitarian Law*, 87 Int'l. Rev. Red Cross 859, 445 (2005) (discussing IW's space/outer space dimensions as well as humanitarian concerns); Jason Barkham, *Information Warfare and International Law on the Use of Force*, 34 N.Y.U. J. Int'l. L. & Pol. 1, 59 (2001) (arguing that an IW attack, used as prelude to a conventional one, would be a

use of force triggering Article 51's right to self-defense).

[17]   *See* Ellis, *supra* note 2, at 6 (rightly recognizing and stating the limitations of U.S. information operations, while acknowledging that "current U.S. statutes criminal statutes apply" to these operations). However, it is worth noting the lack of specific statutes. Ellis offered the U.S. Department of Defense's Office of General Counsel as reference; *see An Assessment of International Legal Issues in Information Operations,* (U.S. DEPARTMENT OF DEFENSE, OFFICE OF GENERAL COUNSEL), *available at* http://www.au.af.mil/au/awc/awcgate/dod-io-legal/dod-io-legal.pdf (last visited Nov. 29, 2008) (describing the U.S. military's dilemma in dealing with the international legal implications of IW).

[18]   Although the DoD document mentioned a "companion of domestic legal issues," few U.S. statutes were quoted. However, an interesting perspective on Haiti read: "In October 1993, when the United States was considering broadcasting radio messages to the people of Haiti supporting the return of democracy in that nation, the Office of Legal Counsel of the Department of Justice issued a written opinion to the effect that 47 U.S.C § 502 does

not apply to the actions of U.S. military members executing the instructions of the President acting within his constitutional powers to conduct foreign policy and to serve as Commander-in-Chief of U.S. military forces," at 34.

A remarkable account of the Governors Island agreement, masterminded by former President Jimmy Carter (in concert with the Clinton Administration) on July 3, 1993, reveals that "in the run-up to the [Clinton's] inauguration, Clinton was given an intelligence briefing based on satellite reconnaissance and information from agents in Haiti. He was told that thousands of Haitians were chopping down trees to build an armada of boats so that they could sail to America. Days before his inauguration, he reversed himself and announced he would continue the Bush policy." *See* James Adams, The Next World War (1998), at 81- 84. In hindsight, considering Carter's post- incident reaction and the Haitian Generals' actions following the CNN broadcast, IW had proven to be a "double-edged sword" capable of causing self-inflicted wounds.

Indeed, extradition agreements obligate each party, in certain circumstances, to deliver persons accused of a crime to the other party

for criminal prosecution. Conduct that is
not criminal in the U.S. might be considered
illegal under the laws of foreign nations,
thus exposing U.S. citizens to potential
criminal IW prosecutions abroad. In fact,
according to the DoD Office of Legal Counsel,
the U.S. is a party to more than a hundred
bilateral extradition treaties, as well as to
a *1933 Convention on Extradition*, to which
thirteen nations in the Americas are parties.
As demonstrated above, it would be unfair to
proclaim that there is a total absence of U.S.
statutes *vis-à-vis* IO activities or IW, in a
broader context. But nonetheless, an explicit
corpus juris is still needed.

[19]   *See* Ellis, *supra* note 2, *at* 6-7.

[20]   Here is a case in point: to support the
claim that "the FBI generally has primary
jurisdiction over the investigation of federal
crimes," Maj. Richard W. Aldrich cited 18
U.S.C. § 3052 (1994). The latter statute was
cited in the context of a discussion of IO
activities against financial institutions
(e.g., Wall Street). *See* Aldrich, *supra* note 6.

Moreover, civil penalties are also authorized
by the U.S. Congress: "In 1934 Congress enacted
47 U.S.C. §502, which provides, 'Any person
who willfully and knowingly violates any rule,

regulation, restriction, or condition . . . made or imposed by any international radio or wire communications treaty or convention, or regulations annexed thereto, to which the United States is or may hereafter become a party, shall, in addition to any other penalties provided by law, be punished, upon conviction thereof, by a fine of not more than $500 for each and every day during which such offense occurs.'" *See* Ellis, *supra* note 2, at 35.

21 *See* BOND, *supra note* 2, at 31-33 (setting out three approaches to discuss the potential applicability of Article (2) 4 of the Geneva Convention to offensive IW). In the context of domestic law, references to "the spirit of the law" and "the intent of Congress" may easily serve to replace Bond's taxonomically-accurate use of "intent of the parties" in international law.

22 In essence, a "constitutionally-anchored" argument promises great success, as the evidence consistently points at one time or another to a polarizing situation, in which the Executive's power is aggrandized at the expense of that of the Legislative and/ or the Judiciary, in the name of national security. Simply stated, if the Commander-in-Chief creates, promotes, or fails to avoid a

situation (e.g., the perilously "protected" IW *status quo*) in which Congress and the courts are unable to exercise their constitutional power-sharing functions (or if Congress is knowingly misled by the Executive), then there are grounds to claim IW unconstitutionality. Furthermore, the "power equilibrium" advocated in Montesquieu's ESPRIT DES LOIS (1748) is another case in point. Seemingly, the current state of IW passes neither the Montesquieu test nor the U.S. constitutional threshold of separation of powers. On separation of powers, *see* Neal Katyal, *Internal Separation of Powers: Checking Today's Most Dangerous Branch from Within*, 115 YALE L.J. 2314, 2314–2349 (2006). For a closer look at the current gap between technological innovations and IW regulations, *see* Gary H. Anthes, *New Laws Sought for Information Warfare as Technology Outpaces the Law*, COMPUTERWORLD, June 5, at 1; *see also* Bradley Graham, *Military Grappling with Guidelines for Cyber Warfare: Questions Prevented Use on Yugoslavia*, THE WASH. POST, Nov. 8, at sec. 1A (1999).

Lastly, *see* Neal Katyal & Laurence Tribe, *Waging War, Deciding Guilt: Trying the Military Tribunals*, 111 YALE L. J. 1259, 1259–1310 (2002), at 2317 (arguing that just as

the standard separation-of-powers paradigms
(legislature v. courts, executive v. courts,
legislature v. executive) overlap to produce
friction, so too do their internal variants.
When the State and Defense Departments have to
convince each other of why their view is right,
for example, better decision-making results.
And when there is no neutral decision-maker
within the government in cases of disagreement,
the system risks breaking down). Similarly,
the State Department (e.g., with respect to
strategic IW) and the Defense Department
(e.g., with respect to IO activities) have
an important role to play in ensuring that
U.S. IW practices abide by international
and domestic law, while they protect U.S.
interests abroad and safeguard the homeland
against internal and external threats. It
would be counterproductive not to do so.
[23] *See* Columbia Law Review. Editors, *supra* note 6,
at 1074 (arguing that perhaps because of the
widespread and long-standing use of espionage
and because of the legally uncertain connection
between an apprehended spy and the sponsoring
nation, espionage of itself does not appear
to constitute a violation of international
law). The authors also commented that "there
is no apparent reason why reconnaissance and

espionage activities should not be given similar treatment," at 1074.

However, a cardinal difference exists: Although espionage is often buttressed by the failure of nations to protest or demand reparations against apprehended spies, the activities that may be conducted by an overreaching Executive, such as warrantless wiretaps, illegal detention/classification of "high value" intelligence targets, and other suspicious activities have been contested at various levels by several nations.

As the lines of attack continue to blur between individual targets (e.g., persons who may claim privacy and human rights violations) and foreign states (foreign governments and their assets), the general public is likely to turn against what is perceived as a deliberate attempt by corrupt "cyber warriors" to use cyberspace and outer space as means of encroachment on (1) civil liberties, (2) the national integrity of foreign nations, (3) democratic political processes and activities, and (4) other branches of government.

[24] *See* Bert-Jaap Koops, *Cybercrime Legislation in the Netherlands*, Cybercrime and Security, 4, 1-20 (2005); Peter Grabosky, Russel Smith, &

Gillian Dempsey, *Electronic Theft*: *Unlawful Acquisition in Cyberspace*, CAMBRIDGE UNIVERSITY PRESS (2001); *see* particularly, Susan Brenner & Bert-Jaap Koops, *Approaches to Cybercrime Jurisdiction*, 4 J. HIGH TECH. L. 1, 7 (2004) (outlining various approaches, by indicating when States claim jurisdiction and which factors influence that claim). Brenner & Koops's survey covered Belgium, Germany, the Netherlands, Malaysia, Singapore, the Australian state of Tasmania, the Council of Europe's Cybercrime Convention, as well as several U.S. state and federal laws; *see also Draft Convention on Cybercrime*, EUROPEAN COMMITTEE ON CRIME PROBLEMS AND COMMITTEE OF EXPERTS ON CRIME IN CYBER-SPACE, Explanatory Note (June 29, 2001), *available at* http://conventions.coe.int/treaty/EN/projets/projets.htm (last visited Sep. 17, 2008). Ulrich Sieber, *Legal Aspects of Computer-Related Crime in the Information Society*, THE EUROPEAN COMMISSION (1998), *available at* http://www.ag.gov.au (last visited Feb. 12, 2009); for an Asian perspective, *see* Lee Joo-Hee, *Law enforcement officers step up efforts to tame cybercrime*, THE KOREA HERALD, Nov. 17, 2000; Christopher Heath, *Intellectual Property Rights in Asia: Projects, Programmes and Developments*, *available at* http://www.

intellecprop.mpg.de/Online-Publikationen/
Heath-Ipeaover.htm (last visited Oct. 22,
2008); *Philippine President Signs Law to
Punish Computer Crimes*, N. Y. TIMES, June 15,
at Technology section (2000).

Separately, *see* UNITED NATIONS, THE UNITED NATIONS
DISARMAMENT YEARBOOK 362-365(2006) (reviewing the
UN General Assembly Resolutions (UNGA53/70
through UNGA60/45)).

[25]   These legal sources date back to the time
of Cicero, passing through the works of
Justinian I of Byzantine times and the Codex
Theodosianus of *Theodosis II* (408-450) all
the way up to academic productions still in
progress around the world. Meanwhile, the works
of Grotius, Aquinas, Augustine, Montesquieu,
Rousseau, Jenks, and von Clausewitz (some
more controversial than others) have been
particularly useful to the author's own,
independent philosophical approach.

[26]   *See* Katyal & Tribe, *supra* note 22, at 1259.

[27]   *Id.* at 1259; *see also* Marbury *v.* Madison, 5
U.S. (1 Cranch) 137, 163 (1803) (arguing that
the government of the United States has been
emphatically termed a government of laws, and
not of men).

[28]   Hamdan *v.* Rumsfeld, 542 U.S. 507 (2004)
(reversing the dismissal of a habeas corpus

petition brought on behalf of Yaser Esam Hamdi, a U.S. citizen being detained indefinitely as an "illegal enemy combatant." Although the Court recognized the "power" of the Executive to detain unlawful combatants, the ruling against the government contends that detainees who are U.S. citizens must have the ability to challenge their detention before an impartial judge); *see also* Hamdan *v.* Rumsfeld, 344 F. Supp. 2d 152 (D.C. Cir. 2004); Hamdan v. Rumsfeld, 415 F.3d 33 (D.C. Cir. 2005).

[29] WILFRED C. JENKS, THE COMMON LAW OF MANKIND (1958); *see also International Law and Activities in Space*, INT'L. & COMP. Q. 5, 92 (1956).

[30] The "voluntarism" of Dutch philosopher Hugo Grotius (1583-1645) postulated "human will" as the supreme manifestation of reality. In international relations, similarly, it is the "will" of individual Member States ("their voluntary participation" safeguarded by national sovereignty) that often delays international consensus on several major *dossiers*, thus calling, in the present context, for a transcendental juridical notion of IW (e.g., a notion that carries broad appeal among heterogeneous legal traditions). On a separate note, Grotius's overall natural law movement often clashed

with certain humanitarian principles, such
as the subtle distinction between choice and
free choice. For example, Grotius's stance on
slavery remains controversial to the point of
being qualified as incompatible with human
rights. For instance, connecting Grotius
to Seneca, Montesquieu "did not excuse his
French" when he reproached the former in the
following terms: "En somme, Grotius ne marque
aucune désapprobation pour l'esclavage. Il
l'accepte comme de droit naturel, 'sinon
de conscience.'" [In sum, Grotius failed to
condemn slavery. He accepts it to be of natural
law 'or as a matter of conscious choice.'].
Simply put, Montesquieu decried Grotius's
stand on voluntary contractual slavery. *See*
Russells Parsons Jameson, Montesquieu et l'esclavage : Etude
sur les origines de l'opinion anti-esclavagiste en France
au XVIIIe siecle, (1971), at 152. On Seneca,
see Keith R. Bradley, *Seneca and Slavery*, 37
Classica & Mediaevalia 161, 161 (1986).

[31] This "redefinition" process does not happen
without major foreign policy shifts, which
often trigger regional conflicts and even wars.
The examples are not limited to the rise of
Iran in the Middle East and the controversial
shifts by some former Soviet republics in
Eastern Europe (e.g., the Russia-Georgia

incident also known as the "2008 Caucasus Conflict"). For instance, Brazil and Venezuela have been under constant pressure, as they emerge as promising technology pioneer and oil "powerhouse" in Latin America. According to a broader international perspective, the growing influence of China, India, Iran, and Russia has created forces with which the international community should reckon. *See* ALVIN TOFFLER, THE THIRD WAVE (1991) (warning of revolutionary technological breakthroughs that would cause "waves" of socioeconomic change).

32   On March 26, 1975, the *Biological and Toxin Weapons Convention* entered into force. The Convention is an indispensable legal and political instrument that reinforces the widespread condemnation of biological weapons. It complements the Geneva Protocol, which banned biological warfare methods in 1925. Accounting for other factors (e.g., military necessity and the dual-use dichotomy), it took nearly fifty (50) years (1925-1975) to come up with what still remains a weak agreement. *See* UNITED NATIONS, THE CONVENTION ON THE PROHIBITION OF THE DEVELOPMENT, PRODUCTION AND STOCKPILING OF BACTERIOLOGICAL (BIOLOGICAL) AND TOXIN WEAPONS AND ON THEIR DESTRUCTION, UNITED NATIONS (1972).

Separately, the U.N. Security Council is still struggling with the Non-proliferation Treaty. The lesson to be learned is that a weak domestic foundation very often translates into weak international conventions and treaties. Of course, international conventions that are rooted in pre-existing domestic legal regimes are inherently stronger. There is no doubt of the fact that the international community awaits explicit and strong IW regulations. Today's "Information Society" cannot afford anything less, under IW's peculiar and interstellar threats of PWMD.

33   Jean Deglaire, La notion juridique du dommage de guerre 25, 35 (1920), trans., [The juridical notion of war damage].

34   Louise Doswald-Beck, *Some Thoughts on Computer Network Attack and the International Law of Armed Conflict*, 76 Int'l L. Stud. 163, 163 (2002); see Byard Q. Clemmons, *Cyberwarfare: Ways, Warriors and Weapons of Mass Destruction*, 79 Mil. Rev. (Oct.-Sept.) 5, 34-35 (1999) (asserting that computer network attacks can be considered to be means of mass destruction); see also William J. Bayles, *The Ethics of Computer Network Attack*, xxxi Parameters-U.S. Army War College Q. 1, 44 (2001) (citing Russian views on broad offensive use of IW weapons).

35 When virtual conduct is involved, a "de-virtualization" process is needed in order to comply with Deglaire's rules of certainty and the materialization of war damages (e.g., using material facts, involving real people and "quantifiable" destruction or degradation of assets, which may arise out of misconduct and/or crimes).

36 Air Force Policy Directive (AFPD) 51-4, *Compliance with the Law of Armed Conflict*, USAF Pub. para 1.6.1 (1993).

37 *See* Schmitt *et al.*, *supra* note 2, at 1; *see also* Ellis, *supra* note 2; DiCenso, *supra note* 2, at 87-89.

38 *See* Schmitt *et al.*, *supra* note 2, at 1.

39 *See* DiCenso, *supra note* 2, at 88.

40 *See* Berg P. Hyacinthe & Larry R. Fleurantin, *Initial Supports to Regulate Information Warfare's Potentially Lethal Technologies and Techniques*, 3rd Int'l Conf. on IW & Sec. 201 (2007), at 206-207 (establishing the taxonomy of lethal information technologies over a spectrum nearing interstellar reach).

41 *See supra* note 2 (providing a list of legal experts on the topic).

42 *See supra* note 6 (listing various versions of these international instruments).

43   *See* Joint Security Commission, *Redefining Security: A Report to the Secretary of Defense and the Director of Central Intelligence*, at Chap. 8. (Feb. 28 1994), *available at http://www.gao.gov/cgi-bin/getrpt?GAO-05-988R* (last visited Feb. 14, 2009).

44   For example, during the month of June 1998 (and later in February 1999), the Director of Central Intelligence (DCI) testified in Senate hearings that several governments now recognize that computer attacks against civilian computer systems represent an option that foreign enemies could use to 'level the playing field' during an armed crisis against the United States. For more on these U.S. challenges, *see* Kanuck, *supra* note 2, at 272.

45   Even in cases where — enemy — military planners would delay the "demilitarization" of critical civilian infrastructures for strategic reasons, consistent with international laws and treaties, *de lege lata*, humanitarian concerns ought not to be ignored.

46   Mark R. Schulman, *Discrimination in the Laws of Information Warfare*, 37 Colum. J. Transnat'l. L. 939, 939-940 (1999) (arguing that, in reality, the laws of war have long restrained its legitimate conduct. These constraints include distinctions between campaign and

non-campaign seasons and they guide the selection of methods, of weaponry and of targets. They provide specific immunities for certain places and targets. They distinguish between combatants and non-combatants, between legitimate and illegitimate targets. Over the millennia and particularly the past half-century, these rules have expanded and been codified in international law).

Did Schulman's argument include IW conducts, weapons and "capabilities"? His abstract clearly stated: "As societies and economies increasingly rely on electronic telecommunications, they grow more vulnerable to threats from other computer systems. At the same time, state's military and intelligence organizations are increasingly developing the capability to attack and defend these assets," *supra*, at 939.

47 JEAN PICTET, HUMANITARIAN LAW AND THE PROTECTION OF WAR VICTIMS, 28-29 (1975), trans., [LE DROIT HUMANITAIRE ET LA PROTECTION DES VICTIMES DE LA GUERRE] (calling for, according to Law of Armed Conflict, mitigation of human suffering and painless healing, as public opinion tended to weigh in then, as it weighs in now, in winning or losing any war).

48 *See* Ellis, *supra* note 2 (warning that current U.S. criminal statutes apply to IO). Despite Col. Ellis's warning, the need for an explicit

IW *corpus juris* has yet to be met. Thus, if applicable U.S. statutes do exist, they are unlikely to be explicit enough to invalidate the concerns of Prof. Schmitt, Maj. DiCenso, Maj. Ramey, Prof. Wingfield, and Col. Ellis.

[49] *Id.* at 6-8; *see also* DoD Office of General Counsel, *supra* note 17 (wherein several U.S. statutes — albeit not with specific enough terms — had been cited); *see also* *DoD Directive 2311.01E*, (DEPARTMENT OF DEFENSE, May 9, 2006), *available at http://*www.dtic. mil/whs/directives/corres/html/231101 (last visited March 20, 2009) (Members of the DOD component comply with the law of war during all armed conflicts, however such conflicts are characterized, and in all other military operations).

The allegations (of war crimes) alone could tarnish a government's reputation and that of its military personnel. For example, individuals accused of war crimes often find it difficult to travel abroad.

[50] This approach postulates a foundational domestic law paradigm, which is built on the synergistic exhibition of three universal legal tenets: *conduct, damage,* and *responsibility.* Juxtaposed with this approach is the international "normative frame of reference," which is

accepted as an applicability test apparatus, particularly, through judicial analogies drawn on the *Geneva Conventions of 1949 (I-IV)* and the *Additional Protocols of 1977(I-II)*. Even certain principles found in the *Hague Conventions of 1899 (I-IV)* and *1907 (I-XIV)* may play a role in tracing international parties' historical intent to draw a line between *jus ad bellum* and *jus in bello*.

III. Domestic, International, and Interstellar Implications

The IW paradigm is also taking a perilous interstellar dimension — an especially disturbing development as IW laws are still needed to punish war crimes or address other pressing humanitarian concerns swiftly.[51] This Section examines the legal implications of involving WMD, and offers initial suggestions for the regulation of the most lethal information technologies of the new millennium; it concludes with a review of existing laws that bind the U.S.

In a broader context, the author acknowledges the need to strike a fine balance between humanitarian concerns and military necessity, with respect to domestic, customary and international laws. With this concern in mind, he conjugates lethality as well as physicality of IW technologies and techniques, the involvement of IW in "armed conflicts," the on-going initiative by U.S. military officials to address humanitarian concerns and potential charges of war crimes,[52] and the military necessity to protect critical infrastructures (e.g., communications satellites, military bases, warships, and other crafts) from IW.

Domestically, IW plays a quintessential role in strategic defense and security, but it is not only U.S. law that may apply to IW. To the contrary, many scholars argue that foreign criminal statutes will most likely apply to crimes committed during U.S. information operations.[53] Conversely, others suggest that "information attacks" occur in another dimension, cyberspace, to which current law is not applicable.[54] In either case, the asymmetrical nature of IW makes any attempt to maintain "information dominance" very ambitious.[55] Moreover, the ambiguous state of IW law,[56] once perceived as an advantage since States could do as they wished, has now become a threat to the U.S., the entire international community, and even beyond (e.g., outer space and celestial bodies).[57]

Synopsis of IW's Domestic Law Approach

The international legal implications of IW weapon technologies are undeniable.[58]

Nonetheless, the nature of international law suggests it is problematic as the primary source of regulation, in light of its "intentional ambiguities" and its "inflexion" to political pressure. As established above, domestic law has its own flaws, but it also has the advantage of an abundant body of precedent cases on which to draw. Precedent cases will be invaluable in crafting a relevant, up-to-date judicial IW framework rooted in domestic law. International IW regulations are likely to follow "established" domestic IW principles via the international community's traditional "norm-setting" protocols and apparatuses (e.g., during U.N. negotiations in Geneva and New York) — but domestic law should be the starting point.

Synopsis of IW's International Law Approach

Discussions surrounding the international legal implications of IW are relatively new but very fluid. This debate goes beyond transnational law, a broad category which includes all law which regulates actions or events that transcend national frontiers.

Nowadays, when computers and computer systems may be seen as "arms," it is becoming more difficult to deny that IW basically entails technology-based strategies and interstellar weapons that should fall within the law of armed conflict. There is even talk of "lethal information technologies," which have taken an unrestrained interplanetary course.[59] Many legal scholars have been calling for Rules of Engagement that would govern IW in particular, and would take into consideration the applicable law of armed conflict.[60]

Jason Barkham, supported by several experts, invoked Articles 51 and (2)4 of the UN Charter:

> Many types of IW attacks will fit comfortably within the framework of Articles 2(4) and 51. Strategic level IW would be a clear violation of Article 2(4); launching an all-out war, which would cause widespread damage and significant casualties, certainly would trigger the victim's right of collective self-defense. Similarly, if the IW attack were a prelude to a conventional one, it, too, would be a use of force triggering Article 51's right to self-defense.[61]

Summing up, the domestic law approach is appealing because it aptly fits the nature of IW. Throughout the history of mankind, the law has been considered as a "synergistic judicial exhibition of three core elements — conduct, damage, and responsibility — to maintain social order and render justice."[62] Even ancient philosophers made their case in terms of cause and effect. Moreover, when it comes to defining responsibility, authors of religious texts have offered controversial interpretations of good and evil — interpretations that may be relevant, for example, to the psychological warfare strategies adopted on both sides of the so-called war on terror. And in a more modern context, jurors in many Anglo-American trials deal with the adjudication of guilt and declaration of innocence, and conservatives and liberals (including conservative and liberal judges) take contrasting stances on crime and punishment. Certainly, as a matter of law, IO planners ought to account for conduct, collateral damages, and responsibilities resulting from the use of IW weapons and techniques, and the proposed domestic law paradigm has long-standing, well-developed approaches and conceptual frameworks that can be applied.

Synopsis of IW's Interstellar Dimension

Subsequent to China's successful test of a direct-ascent ASAT missile against one of its weather satellites in January 2007, Marine Gen. James Cartwright, vice chairman of the Joint Chiefs of Staff confirmed that the U.S. military had successfully downed its own crippled spy satellite on February 21, 2008: an action interpreted by certain observers as a response to China's ASAT test. With China's apparent successful "extra vehicular spacewalk," the number of U.S. rivals in this arena continues to rise. The pressure is on and China's IW capabilities are significant.

Professor Thomas C. Wingfield of Georgetown University Public Policy Institute identified three types of offensive information operations in space: intelligence collection, offensive operations through satellites, and offensive operations against satellites.[63]

These satellites, vital and vulnerable nodes, have become "high-value targets" for future conflicts in the Information Age. Consequently, world leaders have very few remaining options: (1) introduce secret and dangerous weapons into space to protect their satellites against blinding, shutdown, movement, destruction, and impressments — through space weaponization, in potential violation of existing international laws or (2) establish some form of "interstellar convention" that would explicitly forbid any form of WMD in space — a much needed initiative for international peace and the safeguard of human survival beyond Earth's capillary boundaries. It is rather ultra-hypocritical to talk about ecology and "green everything," while pursuing these arrogant self-destructive interplanetary ambitions — e.g., weaponizing and polluting space and outer-space, which must compel many observers to call into question any sense of remorse displayed, perhaps for political reasons by some, over what has already been done to Earth: the booming digital pollution is far more threatening than the carbon-based disaster.

According to existing international law (e.g., Outer Space Treaty 1967), space is restricted to peaceful use ("peaceful purposes"). Theoretically, no weapons should be allowed in space. Therefore, no armed conflicts should be anticipated in space. In practice, however, since no formal definition was given to the term "peaceful purposes," the installation of defense weapon systems in space could creatively be disguised as an "activity conducted for peaceful purposes."

Professor Wingfield evaluated the legality of offensive information operations in space according to three space treaties. It is worth revisiting some of the key elements below:

The first of these is the Outer Space Treaty. In its preamble, it describes "the common interest of all mankind in the progress of the exploration and use of outer space for peaceful purposes."[64] Space was further identified as the province of all mankind, and, therefore, not subject to sovereign claims by any nation. And with regard to WMD, Article 4 of the Outer Space Treaty details specific prohibitions: weapons of mass destruction anywhere in space, military bases, weapons testing, and maneuvers on the surface of any celestial body.

The second major space treaty is the Liability Convention, which sets a liability standard for activities in outer space, provides an exception to that standard, and details the procedures for pursuing a claim.

The third major treaty is the INTELSAT agreement, which governs the use of INTELSAT communications satellites linking fixed ground stations. In essence, the "neutrality principle" can be very challenging in this case. According to Wingfield "many stationing arrangements, such as the Status of Forces Agreements (SOFAs) the U.S. has with numerous allies, have provisions on the coordination required to launch offensive (distinct from 'aggressive') operations from the host country's soil."[65] As such, national security might forever be intertwined with space security and what could be considered as future "interstellar regulations."

Unfortunately, the international community has been virtually absent in on-going discussions leading up to the eventual regulation of IW's lethal technologies and techniques. And the consequential lack of intellectual and institutional "diversity" is likely to hinder efforts to broker a broad international consensus.

At any rate, it would be very unfair to blame this failure on the "so-called" American hegemony. International scholars seem to keep their distance (voluntarily and willingly). Lessons learned from the successful establishment of previous international instruments (e.g., the Biological Warfare Convention of 1972; The Chemical Warfare Convention of 1993) suggest that, very restricted programs ran by a few military schools, would lack the degree of legitimacy and diversity required to prepare the doctrinal landscape for an international convention on IW's most lethal weapons. Although many foreign military programs have been designed to keep track of this fluid situation, military constraints do not allow the same level of engagement afforded by non-military scholars (whose positions do not necessarily or officially engage government officials). Therefore, until a very broad international consensus is reached, it would be premature (and even dangerous) to assume that lethal IW weapons (not specifically prohibited) are tacitly permitted.

A close-up examination of the rapid evolution of the IW paradigm raises serious concerns regarding its deadly mutations. With regard to "physical destruction," the U.S. Chairman of the Joint Chiefs of Staff defined Command and Control Warfare (C2W) as:

> [T]he integrated use of operations security, military deception, psychological operations, electronic warfare, and physical destruction, mutually supported by intelligence, to deny information to, influence, degrade, or destroy adversary command and control capabilities, while protecting friendly command and control capabilities against such actions. Command and control warfare is an application of information operations in military operations.[66]

Col. Yuan Zelu's earlier description succinctly, but clearly, illustrates IW's interstellar dimension, which concerns many analysts within the international intelligence community.[67] As established above, there are well-known strategic advantages to a military's ability to launch missiles from outer space. Indeed, there is a need for explicit IW regulations to address these growing interplanetary threats.

Taxonomy of Lethal Information Technologies

The physical dimension, rarely and sometimes ambiguously covered in IW literature, involves physical equipment/weapons and human casualties. While software "programs" generally run on physical machines, basic instructions (e.g., lower-level "programs") are required to "boot" a computer — chicken-and-egg dilemma. It is not always a virtual situation.

Of course, there is evidence of previous attempts to conceal the obvious computer-weapon nexus established in this Essay. It is equally important to note that the binomial software/hardware approach is indispensable to capture a full picture of the 21st century battlefield.

Table II illustrates various embodiments (soldiers, weapons, munitions, means of delivery, and "decision-makers") of IW technologies and techniques. The resulting taxonomy (1=least; 6=most) is in-line with earlier efforts deployed at the U.S. National

Defense University around the continuum of physical destructiveness.[68]

Table II. Taxonomy of Lethal IW Weapons

Category	Function	Descriptor	Theater of Application	
			In Use/Used	Anticipated Use
Computer-weapon Singularity (banned weapons) ↑ 6	Fuse available technologies into supra weapon system	Catalyst, Mixer, and Amplifier	No information available	Fusion of conventional, unconventional, and banned weapons. The "interstellar" theater cannot be ignored
Vector-based (emergent weapons) ↑ 5	Cause sensory injuries (e.g., a computer-generated laser bean can be lethal)	Spectrum	Acoustic (non-lethal use in ancient Israel, Panama, and Peru to deceive the enemy); other applications include luminescent and microwave.	Next-generation electromagnetic pulse weapons
Unmanned vehicle-based (shooter) ↑ 4	Handle high-risk missions while conducting surveillance to engage and kill the enemy	All-in-One	Military drones (e.g., Predators, Global Hawk, Shadows, Hunters, Ravens) in Yemen, Iraq, Afghanistan, and elsewhere	Micro and Nano UAVs fully integrated in network centric warfare (e.g., urban warfare and counterinsurgency).
Delivery-associated (weapon system) ↑ 3	Support and guide delivery of payloads	Channel	Telemetry instruments, signals, and related equipment (e.g., satellites). Active in most modern theaters	Bio-inspired weapon systems (hardware and software "auto-regeneration")
Munitions-based (bullets and warheads) ↑ 2	Augment precision and increase lethality	Munitions	Smart bullets and binary weapon systems (e.g., multi-stage delivery systems in various theaters).	DNA-specific load for a new class of weapons
Persuasion-based (gang leader or head of rogue states) ↑ 1	Call to suicide and martyrdom (based on persuasive digital information technologies)	Persuader See Captology of B.J. Fogg, Stanford University	Video (Web and TV) messages directly linked to suicide, martyrdom, and other forms of violent acts	Planted chips (hardware) and Trojan horses (software)

Psychological IW Illustrated: Assault on Obama

Welcome to 21st century psychological IW in American politics and government! The following examples are limited to Barack Obama for the sole purpose of underlining the hidden national security threats associated with vicious attacks against a Commander-in-Chief during wartime. Nevertheless, it is important to note that, psychological IW operations are routinely conducted by operatives on both sides of the political spectrum.

It has been widely reported that seven former CIA directors who served both Republican and Democratic presidents have asked President Barack Obama to end the Justice Department's criminal probe into the harsh interrogations of terror suspects during the Bush Administration. Of course, there is a sharp difference between bipartisanship and "tag-teaming." Most media outlets covered the story, including worldwide Internet activities. The resulting psychological IW impact must have been anticipated by the instigators, given their background.

It is rather scandalous and even disturbing for a group of seven former CIA directors to launch an overt psychological IW campaign against a sitting President. In theory, deprived of the agency's latest actionable intelligence items, the former CIA directors remain very intelligent "outsiders" without all the facts. Therefore, their attempt to create friction between the President and his Attorney General comes across as malicious, disrespectful, and suspicious at best. Further, their effort constitutes a clear act of intimidation directed at the career prosecutor, John Durham, in charge of the new probe. The President would severely impede the Attorney General's ability to proceed at the Justice Department, if he were to fall into this visible trap. The former CIA directors are in a position to know that they can always plead for pardon in favor of any CIA officer, at a different stage of the process, which would be more appropriate — if it were to come down to that. They should have been concerned about potential obstruction of justice allegations and possible waiver of their immunity, for engaging in conducts intended to suppress a probe that might lead directly or indirectly to some of them. Sadly, their "class action" style intervention is consistent with the general perception in

Washington today: you can throw anything at the President.

It was not long ago that Director Leon E. Panetta reported the existence of a sleeper cell or "secret unit" established inside the CIA prior to his arrival. The secret unit remained undisclosed during part of his tenure. According to declassified records, the secret unit intended to operate outside the scope of Director Panetta, and as such, would be free from any congressional oversight: a real danger to the national security of the United States, given previous attempts to integrate "foreign elements" into some of these top security programs.

In addition to the fact that Mr. Panetta was not briefed on the existence of the secret unit, it was not reported until the very probe contested by the former CIA directors became imminent. The former CIA directors' unprecedented action compels many analysts to pose the following questions: Is it common practice at the CIA for departing directors to establish their own, independent sleeper cells, in complicity with obsessed politicians? If not, why do the former CIA directors attempt to minimize this grave assault simultaneously targeting the White House, the U.S. Congress,

and the current CIA director, through their
historic protest? Does the reputation of a
few rogue agents warrant more protection than
that of the entire agency? How many pieces
of new evidence do the former CIA directors
require to justify the need for a new probe
or accept the legitimacy of the Attorney
General's decision? Should the following items
be ignored altogether?

- Newly busted secret unit
- New revelations pointing to possible
  interference with previous probes
- Newly admitted failure of full disclosure
  to Congress
- New discovery of prior warnings *vis-à-vis*
  the legality of certain practices
- New evidence pointing to condescending
  disregard for opposing legal opinions
- Recent disclosure of activities that
  reportedly went beyond authorized
  tactics.

It is not without significance that three
of the ex-directors who signed the letter sent
to the White House worked under President
George W. Bush. The letter included the
shallow argument that follows:

If criminal investigations closed by career
prosecutors during one administration can
so easily be reopened at the direction
of political appointees in the next,
declinations of prosecution will be rendered
meaningless."[69]

With all due respect to the former
directors, when seven of the best in American
intelligentsia reduce this widely anticipated
probe down to a closed case "easily reopened
at the direction of political appointees,"
their motivation must be scrutinized.

Further, given the noticeable link
that exists between the establishment and
retention of secret unit(s) inside the CIA,
the engagement in conducts that went over and
beyond the Bush-era "borderline legal" regime
of harsh interrogation tactics, and the
level of concealment or cover-up concocted
to keep the most dangerous practices hidden
from congressional oversight and the current
CIA Director, there is enough substance for
any wary analyst to rebuke the former CIA
directors' atypical intervention as very
misleading and threatening to the safety
or national security of the United States.

Hence, for the safety of future U.S. presidencies and the respect due to all incoming CIA directors, this group of CIA elders should have been chief instigators of a wider probe to look into this matter. It is an incongruous maneuver to insinuate and threaten that the probe will stop law-biding CIA professionals from performing their duties as expected in the future. If morale is low at the CIA, as it is supposed to be for some, it is not because of the new probe; it is, rather, because the evidence points to a series of activities that should not have been conducted under the agency's watch, in the first place. The probe apparently seeks to resolve outstanding issues in order to boost morale throughout the agency: this is not the first probe of this nature, and it is unlikely to become the last. Of course, a straightforward rebuttal to the former CIA directors could read:

> This is not the first time an investigation closed by career prosecutors during one administration is reopened at the direction of officials in the next. And it is very unlikely to be the last. But at least, contrary to the activities currently under

investigation — stealthily defended by
the former CIA directors, the Attorney
General's conduct is clearly and irrefutably
consistent with the rule of law.

As the author has argued, there is a
fundamental difference between Director
Panetta's early recommendation against the
probe and the latest request, following the
official appointment of John Durham, by a
cohort of seven former CIA directors to squash
the new probe. By claiming "easily reopened
at the direction of political appointees,"
the former CIA directors carelessly disregard
numerous calls by members of Congress and a
cadre of law-binding, career CIA officials
who have fought against these borderline
legal interrogation tactics for years. For
example, Sen. Patrick Leahy, who favors the
probe, is not a political appointee. The
protection of a few "bad apples" — as some
critics would say — should not be given
priority over the integrity of the agency:
America's acquaintance with the rule of law
should not be comprised. Matthew Miller, a
Justice Department spokesman, reminded the
ex-directors that the Attorney General's
decision to order a preliminary review into

this matter was made in line with his duty to examine the facts and to follow the law.

Hypothetically, if a former CIA-director were to conspire with political leaders of one administration to run their own "CIA" inside the CIA, through a secret unit, according to a willing and willful scheme to sabotage the next administration, the traitors and their co-conspirators would have been dealt with according to the rule of law, as opposed to the personal "feelings" of seven former CIA directors. In fact, the former CIA directors do not speak for the CIA.

Thus, it is not surprising that the current and official position of the agency reflects a different reality: the CIA is fully cooperating with the new probe. The CIA was established under the National Security Act of 1947 to collect, correlate, evaluate and disseminate foreign intelligence and counterintelligence and to perform such other functions related to intelligence as the National Security Council directs. As such, it is not "as seen on TV:" the CIA is governed by statutes.

In principle, unprecedented crimes call for unprecedented investigations and/or punishment: given that the busted secret CIA unit, as the preliminary declassified report suggests, was connected [and would likely report] to an underground political network, undoubtedly implicated in the design, implementation, and/or execution of these harsh interrogation techniques, John Durham's interest in this nexus cannot be discarded.

The "secret CIA unit" episode reveals simultaneously a manifest breach of protocols, an indefensible act of betrayal against Panetta, a consistent pattern of animosity toward Obama, a mockery out of congressional oversight, and a contemptuous disregard for the rule of law. Simply put, this episode unmistakably exposes the mindset in the departing administration, even as power was being transferred from Bush to Obama. Accordingly, many critics have been forced to ask the question that follows. During the White House transition period, was the Obama Administration being briefed or being entrapped? Technically, the departing administration had from Election Day to Inauguration Day to redeem itself in this particular situation.

Now, Congress should look into lawful means to deal with any immunity issues that may arise and allow justice to run its course, fully and swiftly, for it is very difficult to imagine a greater threat to U.S. national security — not even the Nixon nightmare (e.g., Watergate) could measure up to the gravity of the overall "scheme" from which these unthinkable and repugnant conducts have emerged. Swift justice and exemplary sentences, followed by the restoration of law and order inside the CIA, carry great potential to spare the agency from mutating into what many anti-American propagandists would eagerly label as: a state-sponsored, dysfunctional terrorist organization, plagued by self-destructive conducts of competing secret cells, that espouses torture and other inhumane practices.

Limiting this probe to low-ranking field CIA agents would be ironic and unjust, if the high-ranking political figures behind these conducts remain unpunished. Such a scenario would vindicate the former CIA directors' reasoning vis-à-vis the political dimension of this complex issue. Ultimately, however, adopting the "political reasoning" would not be the best option, when it comes to the application of the rule of law advocated herein.

The CIA has been granted enough latitude to perform its duties. CIA agents should not expect to perform such duties at the peril of the agency or in exchange to endangering U.S. national security by breaking U.S. laws or violating international conventions and treaties. The author is not preemptively adjudicating guilt; he is clearly arguing in favor of a widely anticipated probe. Functionally, the buck needs to stop somewhere, to paraphrase President Truman.

What about the unprecedented insults and technology-enhanced tactics of former Governor Sarah Palin, Rep. Joe Wilson, and Rep. Trent Franks?

Speaking at the recent *How To Take Back America Conference*, Rep. Trent Franks declared that nobody should be shocked that President Obama does all sorts of "insane things" because he is an "enemy of humanity." His incendiary comments were later posted on the World Wide Web via You Tube: illustrating thereby the use of digital information technologies to conquer mind and soul in the political arena.

On a separate note, during a Joint Session of Congress, Rep. Joe Wilson shouted: "You lie!" at the President from his seat. Rep. Wilson's insult was an instant Internet hit: confirming the success of unrestricted psychological IW tactics employed against Obama in recent months.

Based on former Governor Sarah Palin's unique "experience," she has reportedly led a group of American seniors into believing that Obama's health plan involved a bureaucratic "death panel" aimed at killing her elderly parents and her infant son suffering from Down Syndrome. Simply stated, as an "enemy of humanity" doing "insane things," to borrow Rep. Trent Franks's verbiage, Obama is supposedly hiding a plan to commit mass murder of American seniors.

Now, though linking innocent African-Americans to crime is not a new deal in America, many observers have been surprised by the level of animosity directed toward Obama, while others simply tell the truth that hurts. For example, according to former U.S. President Jimmy Carter, statements such as calling Obama a "Nazi" are not just "casual outcomes of a sincere debate" over the President's health care proposals. He said it is "deeper than that." During a town hall meeting in the southern state of Georgia, Mr. Carter made the following observation: some Americans feel that an African-American "ought not be President and ought not be given the same respect as if he were white."[70]

It is important to note that Mr. Carter is a Democrat, but he is not an African-American playing the race card. He is not running for office, and he does not seem to be part of Obama's inner circle. If President Obama is forced to run away from addressing the race issue, while African-Americans and other minority groups continue to suffer at the bottom of the socio-economic stratum, not only he will lose support within the African-American and Latino communities, future African-American leaders might be perceived as "too vulnerable" to fight racial discrimination or to narrow the margin of social inequity in America. American voters might feel compelled to look for the next Bill Clinton who will overtly decry racial insults and address their equal opportunity concerns, while maintaining enough support among Caucasian voters to govern effectively. Sitting the first African-American in the White House is not a miraculous cure. How Obama handles this contentious race debate will determine the fate of African-American leaders in American politics and beyond.

Several IW pundits have already called into question the legality of military grade psychological IW operations targeting Americans with secret "logic bombs" at home. Others have concluded that even the most cautiously designed military-based psychological IW campaign, launched against a foreign entity, would eventually reach the American audience through continuous international news coverage and ubiquitous Internet links: in potential violation of existing U.S. laws.[71] On the international law level, the military principles of proportionality and distinction ought to be considered.

Though China, Russia, and the United States could not be located on the signatories' list, the closest U.S. allies negotiated the Convention on Cluster Munitions (CCM) based primarily on the following conclusion: these indiscriminate and unreliable weapons pose an unacceptable threat to civilian populations during and long after combat operations have ceased. On the same note, as Sen. Dianne Feinstein's letter to President Obama suggests, the Obama Administration has been under tremendous pressure to "conduct a thorough review of U.S. policy on cluster munitions."[72]

Hence, it may cogently be argued that the same legal principles employed to prohibit the use of "cluster munitions" in kinetic warfare will likely apply to the cyber warriors' use of indiscriminate "logic munitions" or "digital clusters" in psychological cyber warfare. It can further be argued, as done throughout this Essay, that America is safer with its foothold anchored in the rule of law, while respecting the rights of every citizen, including the President's right to perform his duties regardless of race, religion, or ethnic background.

Existing Laws That Bind the U.S

The FISA Amendments Act of 2008 set forth the legal basis for electronic surveillance in the U.S. pertaining to foreign intelligence. An Act of Congress that amended the Foreign Intelligence Surveillance Act of 1978,[73] it mainly focused on the legality and illegality of intentional electronic monitoring and disclosure of the use of information obtained by electronic surveillance.[74] Violators are subject to a fine of up to $10,000 or up to five years in prison, or both.[75] Electronic monitoring as defined in the statute includes, but is not limited to, monitoring of both email and phone communications.

In parallel, the Wiretap Act of 1968 expressly prohibits any person from illegally intercepting, disclosing, using or divulging phone calls or electronic communications. The Act covers wire and electronic communication interceptions in the United States; a violation is punishable by fine, imprisonment for up to five years, or both.[76] Notably, the Electronic Communications Privacy Act of 1986 (ECPA) amended the Wiretap Act of 1968 and prohibited certain access to, use of, and distribution of wire and electronic communications.

However, the "state secret" defense has been used frequently in recent years,[77] albeit the intent of Congress, thus far, seems to have been consistent with the Fourth Amendment of the U.S. Constitution[78] (including determinations about the ultimate constitutionality of government searches and seizures) when it authorized the establishment of the Foreign Intelligence Surveillance Court (FISC).

Interestingly, the Protect America Act (PAA) of 2007 made several important amendments to FISA, which will affect the FISC. First, the PAA immunized non-governmental third parties such as telecommunications companies from liability for providing information to the government pursuant to either a FISA warrant or a certification by the Attorney General or the Director of National Intelligence that the acquisition of the intelligence or the electronic surveillance being conducted is lawful and that the assistance requested is necessary.[79] Second, it removed the warrant requirement for government surveillance of foreign intelligence targets (including United States citizens) "reasonably believed" to be outside of the United States. [80] Third, Section 2 of the PAA states:

> Nothing in the definition of electronic surveillance under section 101(f) shall be construed to encompass surveillance directed at a person reasonably believed to be located outside of the United States.[81]

A significant case seeking to enforce surveillance laws is *Hepting v. AT&T*, filed in the United States District Court for the Northern District of California in 2006. There, the plaintiffs claim that AT&T unlawfully assisted the government in collecting information about communications routed through AT&T's network; the ACLU has filed similar cases against AT&T and Verizon.[82]

The Alien Tort Claims Act, also known as the Alien Tort Statute (ATS), states: "The district courts shall have original jurisdiction of any civil action by an alien for a tort only, committed in violation of the law of nations or a treaty of the United States."[83] The ATS is notable for allowing United States courts to hear human rights cases brought by foreign citizens. Accordingly, it is likely to be used in future cases involving IW crimes against humanity. However, defendants are likely to argue that it was not the intent of Congress to address the humanitarian concerns — arising out of IW situations — that are raised in this Essay. Within this context, at the intersection of digital information technologies and humanitarian concerns, *Wang Xiaoning v. Yahoo* is the closest case in point.[84] Ultimately, Yahoo settled the suit for an undisclosed amount.[85]

Divided into five titles, the Digital Millennium Copyright Act (DMCA)[86] was signed into law on October 28, 1998. It implements two 1996 World Intellectual Property Organization (WIPO) treaties: the WIPO Copyright Treaty and the WIPO Performances and Phonograms Treaty. The five titles essentially address a number of other significant copyright-related issues:[87]

Title I, the "WIPO Copyright and Performances and Phonograms Treaties Implementation Act of 1998," implements the WIPO treaties.[88]

Title II, the "Online Copyright Infringement Liability Limitation Act," creates limitations on the liability of online service providers for copyright infringement when engaging in certain types of activities.[89]

Title III, the "Computer Maintenance Competition Assurance Act," creates an exemption for making a copy of a computer program by activating a computer for purposes of maintenance or repair.[90]

Title IV contains six miscellaneous provisions, relating to the functions of the Copyright Office, distance education, the exceptions in the Copyright Act for libraries and for making ephemeral recordings, "webcasting" of sound recordings on the Internet, and the applicability of collective bargaining agreement obligations in the case of transfers of rights in motion pictures.[91]

Title V, the "Vessel Hull Design Protection Act," creates a new form of protection for the design of vessel hulls.[92]

Simply stated, the DMCA criminalizes production and dissemination of technology, devices, or services intended to circumvent Digital Rights Management (DRM) measures pertaining to copyrighted materials. The Act also heightens the penalties for copyright infringement on the Internet. Although this legislation will be useful against corporate espionage and other illicit economic intelligence activities, it failed to address certain IW conducts that cause human casualties, or the physical destruction of property. Notably, in sharp contrast to some of the deadly IW conducts described earlier, the DMCA does not seem to cover war crimes and crimes against humanity.

In synthesis, unlike the Geneva Convention or the Law of Armed Conflict (LOAC), these laws do not cover direct involvement in armed conflict nor do they cover physical harm to non-combatants and other types of war damages identified in this Essay. U.S.C Title 50 (War and National Defense) places certain restrictions on intelligence gathering and sharing, but it does not address most the IW concerns discussed in earlier sections. Though U.S.C Title 10 (Armed Forces) seems to wave the pre-approval requirement pertaining to formal declaration of war by Congress, The War Powers Act of 1973 still maintains some form of timely post-deployment notification requirement. As noted earlier, Congress is unlikely to declare perpetual IW involving armed conflicts. Unfortunately, while these laws bind the U.S., they fail to cover some of the most peculiar IW conducts. In the meantime, the space race for "interstellar dominance" is changing the rules of the game in important ways.

The Obama Administration has shown great concern regarding this topic. According to Scott Pace, a former NASA official who heads the Washington-based Space Policy Institute, "The questions [concerning China's ability to design satellites that, once launched, could catch up with and destroy U.S. military and/or commercial communications satellites] are exactly the ones the Obama team needs to ask."[93] Moreover, in a brave policy move to boost cooperation between NASA and the Pentagon, Obama has promised to revive the National Aeronautics and Space Council, which oversaw the entire space arena during the administrations of four presidents, and was most active from 1958 to 1973.[94] Meanwhile, both U.S. law and international law require

military leaders to monitor and ensure that
soldiers (cyber warriors included) use legal
weapons in all operations.[95] Accordingly, Col.
Ellis explicitly warned everyone involved
across domestic and international legal
regimes that such monitoring was necessary.[96]
Even covert IO activities require (legal)
presidential approval.[97] In sum, these laws
bind the U.S. in very interesting ways.[98]

Snapshot at the Super Five's IW Approaches

The five superpowers of the UN Security
Council (Super Five) approach IW according
to their capabilities, needs, and coalition
partners: French cyber warriors are notorious
for their prolific economic intelligence
skills, while their European counterparts
develop very advanced "penetration"
capabilities to exploit insider threats
(Great Britain) and civilo-military networks
(Russia) to dominate in asymmetric strategies
and techniques. Militarily, France is behind
in this IW race, mainly because of its "wild
card" status on the Council. It tends to
"swing" between the two blocks (US-UK and
China-Russia); but France intermittently

benefits from its NATO affiliation as well as its "special" relationship with Germany. The Russians possess an impressive arsenal of electromagnetic pulse (EMP) weapons and participate in several "joint ventures" with China, seemingly, to compete against the US-UK block. The U.S. tops the list with eavesdropping capabilities and intense digital propaganda (e.g., psychological IW), relying mainly on space power. China comes second with "advanced electronics," backed by an aggressive and evolving space program.

It is worth noting Britain's powerful propaganda machine, while signaling China's reservations in this arena. While China, Russia, and France use psychological IW techniques with a certain level of clumsiness, America and Great Britain use them comfortably across the board.

As for legal IW expertise, the U.S. has a rich archive of legal research to build on. However, a large majority of investigations conducted by U.S. military scholars had been unfortunately focused on proving that the rule of law does not apply to most IW conducts. Ambiguity in semantics has often been quoted as the primary inapplicability criterion, even for the most carefully drafted statute under consideration. Today, however, there is an evident paradigm shift underway; but because top U.S. military officials have stood sternly against explicit IW rules of engagement for almost two decades, it will be very difficult for the U.S. to lead in this arena. Hopefully, the U.S. Air Force — the leading authority in IW/IO literature — will revisit the situation and promote explicit IW regulations. France is making significant progress in this arena, though not without opposition and a lack of prior research.

ENDNOTES-III

51 *See* Clemmons, *supra* note 34; Bayles, *supra* note 34; Hyacinthe & Fleurantin, *supra* note 40, at 210; Berg P. Hyacinthe, *Warning to Information Planners: "Ignore the Information Seeking Behavior of Potential Information Warfare Victims to Your Peril,"* 5TH CONFERENCE ON I-WARFARE AND SECURITY 27-34 (2009); Berg P. Hyacinthe, *System and Device for Prevention and Neutralization of Bioactive Substances and Generating an Aroma-producing Substance*, UNITED STATES PATENT AND TRADE OFFICE, US- 60/700,700,708 (2005); Yuan Zelu, JOINT SPACE WAR CAMPAIGNS (2005) (offering a rare look into China's strategic IW ambitions); Berg P. Hyacinthe, *Autonomous Bio-chemical Decontaminator Against Weapons of Mass Destruction*, (HARVARD'S SMITHSONIAN/NASA ASTROPHYSICS DATA SYSTEM, June 2006), *available at* http://adsabs.harvard.edu/abs/2006SPIE.6201E..21H (last visited Feb. 17, 2009).

52 *See* Treadwell, *supra* note 7; *see also* Ellis, *supra* note 2; Aldrich, *supra* note 6; Schmitt, *supra* note 5; Gevena Conventions.

53 *See* Ellis, *supra* note 2.

54 *See* Robbat, *supra* note 2.

[55] For an instructive introduction to this topic, *see* Bates Gill & Lonnie Henley, China and the Revolution in Military Affairs (1996); John Arquilla & Soloman Karmel, *Welcome to the Revolution . . . in Chinese Military Affairs*, 13 Defense Analysis 3, 255 (1997); *see also* Roger C. Molander *et al.*, *Strategic Information Warfare: A New Face of War*, 1996 Rand's National Defense Research Institute, at 83-90; Carol J. Rogers, The Functional Relationship Between Information Operations and Military Intelligence (2001) (U.S. Army War College report exploring strategies applicable to tactical and strategic military operations); *see also* Graham, *supra* note 22, at 6 (exposing the U.S. military's struggle with regulations and guidelines concerning "acceptable" IW conducts).

For an overview of China's strategic information paradigm, *see* Gurmeet Kanwal, *China's New War Concepts for 21st Century Battlefields*, 48 Inst. Peace and Conflicts Stud. 7, 1 (2007) (discussing the active defense doctrine or "jiji fagyu" of China's People's Liberation Army (PLA). Another case in point is China's ambition to conduct a "people's war" under modern conditions or "gaojishu tiaojian xia de jubu zhazheng." *See also* Bayles, *supra* note 34; Toshi Yoshihara, Chinese

Information Warfare: A Phantom Menace or Emerging Threat? (2001); Timothy Thomas, *New Developments in Chinese Strategic Psychological Warfare*, 16 Spec. Warfare, 1, 9 (2003); Kevin Pollpeter, *Motives and Implications Behind China's ASAT Test*, 7 China Brief 2, 2 (2007).

For a perspective on Russia, *see* John Arquilla & David Ronfeldt (eds.), In Athena's Camp: Preparing for Conflict in the Information Age, (1998). *See also* Martin Libicki, What Is Information Warfare? (1996); John Arquilla & David Ronfeldt, *Cyberwar Is Coming,* 12 Comparative Strategy, 2, 141 (1993); Richard Szafranski, *A Theory of Information Warfare: Preparing for 2020*, 9 Airpower J. 1, 56-65 (1995) (warning that [by 2020 or sooner] the United States should expect that its information systems are vulnerable to attack. It should further expect that attacks, when they come, might come in advance of any formal declaration of hostile intent by an adversary state).

[56] *See* Treadwell, *supra* note 7 (questioning the legality of certain IW conduct).

[57] Regina Hagen & Jürgen Scheffran, *Une interdiction des armes dans l'espace est-elle possible? (Is space weapons ban feasible?),*" 1 Institut des Nations Unies pour la Recherche sur le Désarmement : Forum du Désarmement 45, 45 (2003) (describing

legal loopholes and the impending dangers associated with weapons of mass destruction in space); *see also* Hyacinthe & Fleurantin, *supra* note 40, at 203; Zelu, *supra* note 51; Wingfield, *supra* note 2 (discussing exclusion of traditional military activities under 50 U.S.C § 413(e)). *See* Hyacinthe, *supra* note 51, at 31-32 (discussing weaknesses in ongoing "slow motion" debates at the U.N. *vis-à-vis* undeniable IW interplanetary threats); Jed Margolin, *Microwave Transmission Using Laser-generated Plasma Beam Waveguide*, United States Patent Office, US-6,377,436 (2002) (illustrating potential implications of powerful laser applications in the aforesaid pentagonal synchrony of modern warfare theaters).

[58]   *See* Aldrich, *supra* note 6; DiCenso, *supra* note 2; Ellis, *supra* note 2.

[59]   Berg P. Hyacinthe, De la notion juridique de Cyberguerre 12-14 (2008) [On the juridical notion of Information Warfare] (unpublished report presented at Assas School of Law-La Sorbonne in partial fulfillment of LLD requirements); *see supra*, at 14 (stating, "Or, bien que le débat sur les implications légales de la cyberguerre soit déjà entamé, l'accent mis sur les technologies ou « armes » létales qui en dérivent est particulièrement faible et très difficile à repérer," trans.,

[Despite recently open debates concerning IW, there is still a need to address the legal implications of lethal IW technologies or "weapons," and to increase public awareness accordingly]; *see also* Hagen & Scheffran, *supra* note 57, at 53 (illustrating well-known strategic advantages to a military's ability to launch missiles from outer space). One of these advantages, lethally enhanced by several powerful laser applications (e.g., electromagnetic pulse weapons), is a combination of "unbeatable" speed and interstellar reach, allowing access to targets located on land, in the air and sea, and in space and cyberspace. For the taxonomy of lethal IW weapons and techniques, *see* Hyacinthe & Fleurantin, *supra* note 40, at 209. Accordingly, *see* Greenberg et al., *supra* note 2, at 5 (describing "a continuum of physical destructiveness" through earlier efforts deployed at the U.S. National Defense University).

[60] William A. Roig, Creating Rules of Engagement for Information Warfare: Examining the Policy Implications of International Law (1997); Daniel Vadnais, *Law of Armed Conflict and Information Warfare —How Does the Rule Regarding Reprisals Apply to an Information Warfare Attack* (Maxwell AFB#A098293), *available at* https://research.maxwell.af.mil/papers/

ay1997/acsc/97-0116.pdf (last visited Feb. 14 2009); Michael N. Schmitt, *Computer Network Attack and the Use of Force in International Law: Thoughts on a Normative Framework*, 37 Colum. J. Transnat'l L. 885, 929 (1999); Barkham, *supra* note 16; Brown, *supra* note 2; Hollis, *supra* note 3.

61 See Barkham, *supra* note 16, at 80; for experts supporting Barkham's approach, *see* Bond, *supra* note 2; Robert G. Hanseman, *The Realities and Legalities of Information Warfare*, Air Force L. Rev. 42, 173 (1997); Todd A. Morth, *Considering Our Position: Viewing Information Warfare as a Use of Force Prohibited by Article 2(4) of the U.N. Charter*, Case W. Res. J. Int'l L. 567, 595 (1998).

62 *See* Hyacinthe, *supra* note 59, at 7.

63 Wingfield, *supra* note 2, at 1.

64 *See id.* at 6.

65 *See id.* at 9.

66 Memorandum of Policy #30, *Command and Control Warfare*, Joint Chiefs of Staff Publications (1993), at 2.

67 *See* Toshi Yoshihara (2001), Chinese Information Warfare: A Phantom Menace or Emerging Threat? (exploring, from the U.S. Army War College's Strategic Studies Institute, what the author perceives to be China's pursuit of IW as a method of fighting asymmetric

warfare against the U.S. via adaptation and mutation of local flavors), *available at http://www.au.af.mil/au/awc/awcgate/ssi/chininfo.pdf* (last visited Dec. 19, 2008); Gary D. *Rawnsley, Old Wine ...Taiwan Computer-Based 'Information Warfare' and Propaganda*, 81 INT'L AFFAIRS 5, 1061-1078 (2005); Tom Wilson, *Threats to United States Space Capabilities*, (U.S. Space Commission), *available at* http://www.fas.org/spp/eprint/article05.html#8.

[68] GREENBERG *ET AL.*, *supra* note 2, at 5.

[69] Peter Baker, *Former C.I.A. Chiefs Protest Justice Inquiry of Interrogation Methods*, (N.Y. TIMES, Sept. 18, 2009), *available at* http://thecaucus.blogs.nytimes.com/2009/09/18/former-cia-chiefs-protest-justice-inquiry-of-interrogation-methods/?ref=world, (last visited Sept. 30, 2009)(reporting that seven former CIA directors, shortly after Attorney General Eric H. Holder Jr. assigned a career prosecutor, John Durham, to look into the matter, protest the Attorney General's decision in a letter to the White House).

[70] *Carter: Some Obama Opposition Race-Related* (VOA NEWS, Sept. 16, 2009), *available at* http://

www.voanews.com/english/2009-09-16-voa14.cfm
(last visited Sept. 30, 2009)(quoting former
U.S. President Jimmy Carter on rising vocal
attacks against President Barack Obama).

[71] *See* the U.S. Information and Educational
Exchange Act of 1948 (Public Law 402), also
referred to as the Smith-Mundt Act, that emerged
from President Woodrow Wilson's "Committee of
Information" and President Harry Truman's
"Campaign of Truth" programs. The Smith-Mundt
Act was unanimously passed by Congress to
establish the U.S. Information Agency (USIA).
Furthermore, the intent of Congress has been
clearly stipulated through continuous efforts
to shield the American public from the type
of psychological IW tactics aimed at foreign
targets (e.g., Al Qaida members, *et al.*).
From the Smith-Mundt Act to the Zorinsky
Amendment of the 1972 Foreign Relation Act,
Congress has consistently imposed several
restrictions on psychological operations to
avoid "influencing public opinion in the U.S."
and/or "distributing propaganda materials
[authorized for foreign use only] within
the U.S." The Charter of the Presidential
Decision Directive (PDD) 68, *International
Public Information*, also made it clear that
domestic information should be "deconflicted"

and "synchronized" as to abide by the rule of law.

Now, when Gen. David Petraeus held up propaganda materials in the form of glossy photos of the Iraqi national soccer team to "sell unity" to an American TV anchor, stunned legal analysts quickly noted the danger of psychological operations reaching the U.S. audience. In reality, the photos were intended to "neutralize" a ferocious foreign dividing force in-progress at the time: the costly underestimated Iraqi insurgency. Soon thereafter, a new 2008 report by the Defense Science Board recommending the resurrection of Defense Secretary Donald Rumsfeld's notorious Office of Strategic Influence, repackaged with the label "Office of Strategic Communications," was squashed by a wary Congress. It took the Bush Administration a long time to come clean on Iraq, yet many questions still remain unanswered. Former Secretary of Homeland Security Tom Ridge's recent testimony suggests that Gen. Petraeus's conduct signaled a broader psychological IW campaign charily and deliberately designed to target the American audience on U.S. soil. Ironically, this legal disclaimer/warning vis-a-vis military grade psychological operations (PSYOPS) has been in circulation for years: messages must be truthful and must never try to influence an American audience.

[72] *See* Hon. Sen. Dianne Feinstein's letter addressed to President Barack Obama in September 2009, concerning landmines and cluster bombs. In fact, a petition drive, endorsed by 67 national organizations requesting a review of U.S. policy on landmines and cluster bombs, had been forwarded to the President much earlier.

[73] *See* Foreign Intelligence Surveillance Act of 1978 (FISA), Pub. L. No. 95-511, 92 Stat. 1783 (codified as amended at 50 U.S.C. §§ 1801-1811 (2000 & Supp. II 2003) and in scattered sections of 18 U.S.C. (2000 & Supp. III 2003)); *see also* Pub. L. No. 110-261, § 403, 122 Stat. 2436, 2473 (establishing the FISA Amendments Act of 2008).

[74] *See Letter from Attorney-General Alberto Gonzales to Senators Patrick Leahy and Arlen Specter* (CONG. REG. S646-S647, January 17, 2007), *available at* http://graphics8.nytimes.com/packages/pdf/politics/20060117gonzales_Letter.pdf (last visited Feb. 27, 2009) (reporting to Congress that the President has determined not to reauthorize the Terrorist Surveillance Program when the current authorization expires). In other words, the

Bush Administration was forced to discontinue one of its many controversial programs. For a similar case, see DiCenso, *supra* note 2 (citing an earlier scheme during the Vietnam-era to establish an "elaborate, nationwide system with the potential to monitor any and all political expression: no person was too insignificant to monitor; no activity or incident too irrelevant to record).

[75] *See* James Risen & Eric Lichtblau, *Bush Lets U.S. Spy on Callers Without Courts*, NYT, Dec. 16, 2005, at A1(releasing information pertaining to secret warrantless wiretapping by the National Security Agency (NSA) in late 2005). Though this warrantless practice was discontinued in January 2007, other warrantless practices, expressly affecting foreign intelligence monitoring, are currently permitted under 50 U.S.C. §§ 1805a (b).

[76] *See* 18 U.S.C. § 2510 (establishing a nexus between the Wiretap Act and the Omnibus Crime Control and Safe Streets Act of 1968).

[77] *See* Eric Lichtblau & Adam Liptak, *Bush and His Senior Aides Press On in Legal Defense for Wiretapping Program*, WASH. POST, Jan. 28, 2006, at A2; *see also* the Bush Administration's intervention in the *Hepting* case, arguing that

the case should be dismissed under the "state secrets doctrine" because AT&T could not mount a defense without revealing information related to classified information. The government contends that such disclosure could hamper the government's foreign intelligence gathering activities.

[78] *See* United States *v.* Martin, 413 F.3d 139, 152 (1st Cir.), cert. denied, 126 S. Ct. 644 (2005) (reviewing findings of fact for clear error and legal conclusions in Fourth Amendment context); *see also* United Sates *v.* Runyan, 290 F.3d 223, 234 (5th Cir. 2002).

[79] 50 U.S.C. §§ 1805a to 1805c. *See* Protect America Act of 2007, Pub. L. No. 110-55, 121 Stat. 552; *see also* § 101(f) of FISA, 50 U.S.C. § 1801(f) (defining "electronic surveillance" under the statute as "the acquisition by an electronic, mechanical, or other surveillance device of the contents of any wire or radio communication sent by or intended to be received by a particular, known United States person who is in the United States).

Accordingly, as defined in section 101(i) of FISA, 50 U.S.C. § 1801(i), "United States person" means a citizen of the United States, an alien lawfully admitted for permanent residence (as defined in section 1101(a)(20)

of Title 8), an unincorporated association
a substantial number of members of which
are citizens of the United States or aliens
lawfully admitted for permanent residence,
or a corporation which is incorporated in
the United States, but does not include a
corporation or an association which is a
foreign power, as defined in subsection (a)
(1), (2), or (3) of this section.

[80] 50 U.S.C. §§ 1805a (b).

[81] 50 U.S.C. § 1801(f)

[82] *See Hepting v. AT&T* (2006).

[83] 28 U.S.C. § 1350.

[84] Wang Xiaoning *v.* Yahoo (addressing the
humanitarian concerns of a Chinese dissident,
Wang, who used a Yahoo e-mail account to post
anonymous writings to an Internet mailing
list: Yahoo was accused of passing information
to government officials that prompted the
identification and subsequent arrest of Wang in
September 2002); *see also* Miguel Helft, *Chinese
Political Prisoner Sues in U.S. Court, Saying
Yahoo Helped Identify Dissidents*, N.Y. TIMES,
Apr. 19, 2007, at C4; Ariana Eunjung Cha & Sam
Diaz, *Advocates Sue Yahoo in Chinese Torture
Case*, WASH. POST, Apr. 19, 2007, at D1.

[85] *See* Catherine Rampell, *Yahoo Settles with
Chinese Families*, WASH. POST, Nov. 14, 2007, at D4.

86   Pub. L. No. 105-304, 112 Stat. 2860 (Oct. 28, 1998).

87   *See The Digital Millennium Copyright Act of 1998*, (U.S. Copyright Office Summary, Dec. 1998, at 1), *available at* http://www.copyright.gov/legislation/dmca.pdf (last visited Feb. 28, 2009).

88   *See id.* at 1.

89   *See id.*

90   *See id.*

91   *See id.*

92   *See id.*

93   *See* Demian McLean, *Obama Moves to Counter China With Pentagon-NASA Link*, (Wash. Times, Jan. 8, 2009), *available at* http://www.washingtontimes.com/news/2009/jan/08/ (last visited Feb. 28, 2009) (revealing Obama's plan to address the Chinese strategic IW challenge).

94   *See id.*

95   In Article 36 of the Additional Protocol I-API, labeled "New Weapons," the drafters sent a clear signal concerning both applications and applicability of the following rule to new developments of methods and means of warfare (e.g., IW weapons and techniques): "In the study, development, acquisition or adoption of a new weapon, means or method of

warfare, a High Contracting Party is under an obligation to determine whether its employment would, in some or all circumstances, be prohibited by this Protocol or by any other rule of international law applicable to the High Contracting Party." *See also* Haslam, *supra* note 9, at 160, and Ellis, *supra* note 2 (recognizing the judicial value of the customary law of armed conflict as well as the value of the threat of war crime charges and charges of crimes against humanity). For other domestic statutes, *see supra* note 7 (regarding assessment by the DoD Office of Legal Counsel). For an interesting theoretical perspective, *see also* David Luban, *A Theory of Crimes Against Humanity*, 29 YALE J. INT'L L. 85-167 (2004) (discussing war crimes and crimes against humanity).

96   *See supra* notes 36 & 37.

97   Hyacinthe & Fleurantin, *supra* note 40, at 207 (asserting that information operations, by their very nature, may often be conducted as covert actions); *see also* Wingfield, *supra* note 2; DiCenso, *supra* note 2 (citing Capt. Stephen A. Rose, JAGC, US Navy) (defining covert action as an activity of the US government to influence political, economic,

or military conditions abroad, where it is intended that the role of the US government will not be apparent or acknowledged publicly; and warning that covert action intended to influence US domestic political process, public opinion, policies, or media is expressly prohibited).

The notion of obedience to orders constitutes the foundation of military discipline and effectiveness. Although military servicemen and servicewomen who fail to obey the lawful orders of their superiors risk serious consequences (see Art. 90 of the Uniform Code of Military Justice, making it a crime for a military member to willfully disobey a superior commissioned officer and Art. 91, making it a crime to willfully disobey a superior, or Art. 92, taking a stiffer stand), the U.S. Supreme Court held that Navy commanders "act at their own peril" when obeying presidential orders when such orders are illegal. See Little v. Barreme (1804) (involving the "Flying Fish" case, wherein the U.S. Supreme Court held that Navy commanders act at their own peril when obeying presidential orders when such orders are illegal). At issue was an order by President John Adams, issued in 1799 during the brief U.S. war (The Pirate Wars 1798-1800) with France, authorizing the Navy to seize ships bound for French ports.

Under a different jurisdiction (e.g., that of the Court of Military Appeals) on the same subject, *see* United States *v.* Keenan (upholding the principle that the justification for acts done pursuant to orders does not exist if the order was of such a nature that a man of ordinary sense and understanding would know it to be illegal). In summary, though U.S laws remain unclear on the subject of unlawful orders, the overall jurisprudence on lawful (including presidential) orders is lucid, consistent, and well-developed. To cite a famous example, the international jurisprudence reveals that the "I was only following orders" defense did not work at the Nuremberg tribunals following World War II. Similar defense strategies have also failed (domestically and internationally) long after the Nuremberg Trials.

[98] As established above, though a huge gap in coverage still persists, some of the laws currently on the books in the U.S. that might marginally touch on IW include the Foreign Intelligence Surveillance Act (FISA), the Alien Tort Claims Act, and the Digital Millennium Copyright Act. Unfortunately, these

Acts do not even begin to address some of the most lethal information technologies and other interplanetary threats discussed throughout this Essay.

In France, for example, the Hadopi law is the legal mechanism through which government agencies regulate Internet downloads. It was presented to lawmakers at the "Chambre des députés," an equivalent to the U.S. House of Representatives, on February 18, 2009, only to see the original version rejected by the French Constitutional body known as "Conseil Constitutionel," under a cloud of criticisms mainly from the Socialist Party arguing that blocking access to the Internet might indeed be a 'disproportionate measure' nowadays.

Prof. Gilles J. Guglielmi outlined several Hadopi1 flaws: from the influence of special interest groups to invasion of privacy. Many French jurists had been mobilized on Hadopi.

Hadopi2's most popular adjustment involved the requirement of a judge, as opposed to an Hadopi body, to handle litigations regarding blocking access to the Internet, as well as other forms of sanction, with respect to the three-strike rule. According to post-seminar notes from Assas Law, Prof. Geneviève Koubi expresses "due process" concerns over Art.6.

IV. SEPARATION OF POWERS AND POLICY IMPLICATIONS

Currently, IW exists in an anarchic state, a legal limbo or "black hole,"[99] one that challenges the basic principles of law.[100] The lack of statutes regulating IW seems to create an imbalance among the aforementioned three branches of power: exalting the Executive at the expense of Congress and the Judiciary. This state of affairs, not limited to IW, was recently remedied by the U.S. Supreme Court in the *Hamdan* case with respect to the rights of detainees at Guantanamo — indicating that there may be hope for bring the constitutional separation of powers into play here, too.[101] If Congress were to decide to regulate IW, the Supreme Court might well support its statutes, even if the Obama Administration chose to follow the Bush Administration's prior approach regarding, for example, the Foreign Intelligence Surveillance Act (which is quite unlikely) and make claims of exclusive executive power in this area. Such a scenario seems quite plausible, for the legality of unregulated IW activities has already been challenged under international humanitarian law. Two of the most credible asymmetric threats against maintaining this dangerously dysfunctional IW *status quo* include (1) the emergence of multiple military powers with interplanetary reach (2) the surprisingly growing IW capabilities of non-state actors and the so-called terrorist groups (e.g., mastery of technology-assisted psychological warfare and acquisition of sophisticated improvised explosive devices). We must regulate.

The lack of a lexical definition of IW does not and should not justify the current anarchic state of the law in this area. By analogy, the unsettled definition of life and/ or its origin did not and should not prevent the enactment of capital cases legislations. Should capital murder verdicts be nullified for lack of a consensual lexical definition of the origin of life? Should lethal IW conduct, damages, and responsibilities be ignored altogether based on some "lexicographic" technicalities? The answer is a resounding no. The rule of law should always prevail:

where a clear set of definitions is lacking, the law will provide one.[102]

For example, in his seminal work[103] on the procedural theory of justice, Paul Ricoeur discussed responsibility in terms of the fundamentals of human agency (e.g., personal and moral identity). Ricoeur also linked responsibility to the notion of accountability: "to impute an action to someone is to attribute it to him as its actual author, to put it, so to speak, on his account and to make him responsible for it."[104]

As U.S. authorities encourage other national governments to enact effective legislation regarding high-tech crimes, they run the risk of jeopardizing the missions of U.S. military and intelligence personnel who may be stationed overseas to engage in IO.[105] Though the U.S. military's quest for exemption and immunity may proceed through diplomatic channels, cyber warriors' vulnerability to war crime charges and/or crimes against humanity remains constant. Notably, the U.S. Constitution contains no authority for this approach, meaning that a congressional statute or the enforcement of a prior treaty commitment could put an end to it.

Conventional war crime charges, traditionally brought before the International Court of Justice (ICJ), can also be filed, contrary to popular beliefs, under other jurisdictions(e.g., domestic military courts).[106] In addition, the recent International Criminal Court (ICC or ICCt) is a permanent tribunal to prosecute individuals for genocide, crimes against humanity, war crimes, and the crime of aggression. As many analysts predicted, China, India, Russia, the United States, and other Member States have refused to join the ICC for the moment. Nevertheless, perpetrators of IW war crimes would be subject to charges filed under multiple jurisdictions; major travel restrictions would also apply (even for "non-convicted" defendants).

Furthermore, in light of recently-recorded IW activities, the U.S. Constitution's system of separation of powers appears to restrain the Executive from using the military as a means of encroachment upon the spheres of other branches.[107] In the realm of IW, as in other realms, the Constitution's separation of powers should therefore prevent the concentration of power in the Executive, and provide each branch with weapons to fight off encroachment by the other two. As James

Madison put it, "Ambition must be made to counteract ambition,"[108] and this is no less true in the realm of IW than generally.

It is widely accepted that the practice of States represents the best evidence of what reasonable men believe to be lawful and necessary weapons in war.[109] The current state of IW is unacceptably offensive to the high standards of the U.S. military. Now is the time for the U.S. to regulate. But not only the U.S.; Russia, China, Great Britain, France, India, Japan, and other emergent military powers should also reckon with similar domestic legal realities, for virtually every country's legal system must abhor the anarchy that is the current state of IW weaponry. As established earlier, the Executive should not be allowed to "misuse" the noble military necessity principle to circumvent constitutional safeguards or bypass vital international conventions and treaties, which tend to strengthen international relations and serve as a "down payment" on long-lasting peace and security (at home and abroad).

Concurrently, on the international level, further research should explore the applicability of existing conventions and treaties (e.g., the Biological Warfare

Convention (BWC) of 1972, the Outer Space Treaty
of 1967, the International Telecommunication
Convention (ITC) of 1984, and the Chemical
Warfare Convention (CWC) of 1993) to the quiet
fusion of digital telecommunication networks
and bio-microelectromechanical systems (BIO-
MEMS) into potential diffusers, relays, or
transport vehicles of WMD. Realistically,
however, an explicit international convention
on IW weapons and techniques should not be
expected any time soon. Instead, the best
to hope for in the near future is that some
States, such as the U.S., may interpret the
treaties to reach IW and enforce their own
treaty compliance. Even then, as the author
argues, the dangerous gap in IW semantics
(the gap between what is taught in major
defense and military institutions, and what
is expressly stipulated in the law) would
have to be bridged.

Simply put, protecting cyber warriors
against potential charges of having committed
IW war crimes and/or IW crimes against
humanity will require a significant level
of harmony between military instructions and
the letter of the law. Toward this end, the
development of a new area of law (for instance,
interstellar law) might become necessary.[110]

Bearing a distant resemblance to Star Trek's fictional "galactic" rules, interstellar law aligns itself with, but goes beyond, Phillip Jessup's notion of regulation of the actions or events that transcend national frontiers through transnational law.[111] Is there any justification for contemplating a new area of law to be created in this context? According to Professor Mark W. Janis, "Though the quest for a higher law to specify, supplement, or limit the law and power of a state in the name of justice has lasted for thousands of years, the form and substance of that quest — as manifested as the law of nations, international law, transnational law, and cosmopolitan law — has differed."[112] In this respect, interstellar law seems to embody Professor Janis's notion of a distinct "form and substance" that characterizes today's quest for a higher IW law.

With respect to ideal policies, the author presents the following recommendations, in descending order of preference:

1. Ideally, the U.S. military could act through the leadership of the Secretary of Defense and establish explicit IW guidelines. Other countries could then adopt similar solutions under their own systems of

government. This solution could strike an equitable balance between humanitarian concerns and military necessity, thereby protecting military personnel against war crimes and other prosecutions. Else, the Executive, via the Commander-in-Chief, may intervene.[113]

2. As a "second best" option, the U.S. Congress (or its equivalent in another country) could intervene, a scenario that is likely to provoke a showdown between the three branches of power — and a costly one, considering the looming financial crisis and complex international dossiers currently in motion.

3. Finally, but not optimally, citizens in the U.S. and elsewhere could sue to contest alleged encroachments against constitutionally-guaranteed civil liberties and democratic processes. However, the potential involvement of anti-war groups could further complicate the task at hand with slogans such as: "open war," "undeclared war," and "perpetual war."

As Professor Laurence Tribe has noted, certain constitutional clauses require the wary jurist to "confront the recurring puzzle of how constitutional provisions written two centuries ago should be construed and applied in ever-changing circumstances."[114] Tribe followed up on this comment with a reminder that is particularly relevant in the case of IW:

> New technologies should not lead us to react reflexively either way [—] either by assuming that technologies the Framers didn't know about make their concerns and values obsolete, or by assuming that those new technologies couldn't possibly provide new ways out of old dilemmas and therefore should be ignored altogether.[115]

The prescient warnings of Spenser M. Beresford,[116] NASA's general counsel in the 1960's and Gen. Ronald R. Fogleman, Chief of Staff of the U.S. Air Force (during the 1990's) on June 5, 1995 were clear:

> Because exploiting [information systems] will readily cross international borders, we must be cognizant of what the law allows and will not allow. We must have good legal advice as we get into this.[117]

From a military intelligence perspective, domestic law may still apply to IW weapons and techniques. Though international norms are often given a superior value to those of domestic statutes, Professor John A. Radsan, assistant general counsel at the Central Intelligence Agency (CIA) from 2002 to 2004, discussing intelligence activities, acknowledges that domestic statutes impose certain restrictions, where international law seems to leave an exploitable vacuum:

> While individual countries have regulated their intelligence activities through domestic statutes, very few countries, if any, have signed international treaties or international conventions that cover intelligence activities.[118]

Ultimately, the U.S. Constitution is founded on a universal principle that encompasses IW conduct, as well as other forms of conduct: no state-sponsored conduct, including in time of war, shall be placed above the Constitution.[119] The challenge, as illustrated above, is to ensure that this hallowed principle becomes an enforceable reality.

ENDNOTES-IV

[99] Certain classes of IW weapons and their associated conduct are likely to violate U.S. and international laws. And put into the frightening interstellar context, these "unregulated" activities threaten the survival of Homo sapiens beyond Earth's capillary boundaries. *See* Hyacinthe & Fleurantin, *supra* note 40, at 203.

[100] Requiring material facts for guidance as done on the (legislative) level, monitoring cases (executive), and correcting defects (judiciary), *see* Katyal *supra* note 22, at 2317-2319.

[101] *See id.* at 2319 (using the collapse of external checks and balances during the Bush Administration to demonstrate the need for internal ones). Similarly, the current anarchic state of IW is reviewed, herein, to demonstrate the need for explicit regulations, short of which the current IW paradigm risks the demise of the congressional checking function.

[102] *See* ARTHUR RIPSTEIN, EQUALITY, RESPONSIBILITY AND THE LAW (1999)(disavowing "voluntarism" and suggesting that legal practices of responsibility amount to promoting fair terms of interaction); *see also* PAUL RUSSELL, FREEDOM AND MORAL SENTIMENT: HUME'S WAY OF NATURALISING RESPONSIBILITY (1995)

(establishing Hume's superior approach to the narrow utilitarian "economy of threats" theory).

[103] Paul Ricoeur, *The Concept of Responsibility: An Essay in Semantic Analysis, in* THE JUST 13-14 (Mary D. Pellauer, trans., 2000) (providing, via Pellauer's translation of the French author's philosophical perspective, an instructive introduction to the notion of responsibility).

[104] *Id.* at 14.

[105] *See* DoD, Office of Legal Counsel, *supra* note 17, at 34.

[106] *See supra* note 97 (reviewing military misconduct and citing United States *v.* Keenan); *see also* Ellis, *supra* note 2, at 6; Dicenso, *supra* note 2 (debating on the selection of proper jurisdiction from several available options).

[107] *See* United States *v.* Nixon (1974).

[108] James Madison (*aka* Publius), Federalist Papers, 51 (1788) (addressing means by which checks and balances can be maintained within government through the notion of separation of powers). However, it is worth acknowledging the French constitutionalist Charles de Montesquieu's seminal work Esprit des Lois (1748) as the direct source of Madison's

inspiration. For examples of the Executive's encroachments on legislative powers, *see* Youngstown Sheet & Tube Co. *v.* Sawyer (1952) and Dames & Moore *v.* Regan (1981). For instances of congressional encroachments on executive powers, *see* INS *v.* Chadha (1983); Bowsher *v.* Synar (1986); Morrison *v.* Olson (1988); Mistretta *v.* U.S. (1989). Separately, on the topic of congressional immunity, *see* Hutchinson *v.* Proxmire (1979). On the other side of the spectrum, for the first U.S. Supreme Court decision to declare an act of Congress unconstitutional, *see* Marbury *v.* Madison, *supra* note 27. Lastly, for an instance of encroachment on the Judiciary, *see* Ex Parte McCardle 74 U.S. 506 (1868).

[109]   Paul A. Robblee, *The Legitimacy of Modern Conventional Weaponry*, 71 MIL. L. REV. 148 (1977). For implications regarding U.S. (domestic) law, *see* Department of the Army Field Manual 27-10, *The Law of Land Warfare*, U.S. ARMY, par. 34, at 18 (1956).

[110]   Interstellar law would regulate all interplanetary actions or events that affect human society and its expandable environment. Interstellar law would encompass issues such as space/outer space jurisdiction and sovereignty, the interplanetary "transferability" of

terrestrial patent and intellectual property laws, customary laws of interplanetary societies, space traffic rules, the military necessity for weapons in space, the legality of the presence of weapons in space, and the rules that govern space travel and space migration.

[111]   *See* Phillip Jessup, Transnational Law 2 (1956) (defining transnational law, according to the author's Storrs Lectures delivered at Yale Law School half a century ago); *see also* Hyacinthe & Fleurantin, *supra* note 40, at 204 (suggesting that the concept of interstellar law would be similar to Phillip Jessup's notion of transnational law).

[112]   *See* Mark Weston Janis, *The Quest For a Higher Law*, 116 Yale L.J. Pocket Part 317 (2007), *available at* http://yalelawjournal.org/2007/04/07/janis.html (last visited March 15, 2009).

[113]   Parallel pressure "to regulate" would be applied against Member States (rivals and allies alike), in order to mitigate any tactical and/or strategic military "deficiency" which may result from such initiative.

[114]   Laurence Tribe, *The Constitution in Cyberspace: Law and Liberty Beyond the Electronic Frontier*, 51 Humanist 5, 15-21 (1991), *available at* http://www.epic.org/free_speech/tribe.html (last visited March 7, 2009).

115 *See Id.* (emphasis added); *see also* LAURENCE H. TRIBE, AMERICAN CONSTITUTIONAL LAW §12-7 825-832 (2d. ed. 1988) (warning about the "oversimplified" interpretation of the speech/conduct dichotomy in First Amendment context). However, *see* Bergstein v. United Sates Dept. of State (1996) (recognizing, for the first time, a protected speech interest in computer code — labeled then as "defense article" under a controversial "export" rule by the U.S. Department of State).

116 *See* Beresford, *supra* note 6, at 107.

117 *See* FREDRICK OKELLO *ET AL.*, INFORMATION WARFARE: PLANNING THE CAMPAIGN, 6 (1996), *available at* http://fas.org/irp/threat/cyber/96-124.pdf (last visited March 3, 2009).

118 *See*, John. A. Radsan, *The Unresolved Equation of Espionage and International Law*, MICH. J. INT'L L. 28, 597, 595-624 (2007).

119 *See* Tribe, *supra* note 114, at Axiom 4 (asserting that the Constitution is founded on normative conceptions of humanity that advances in science and technology cannot disprove).

V. LIMITATIONS OF THE AUTHOR'S APPROACH

The author's approach contains an important set of limitations: First, it embodies a U.S.-centric perspective. This approach is justified in that the U.S. system possesses many of the characteristics that illustrate why a domestic law approach is superior. Also, the U.S. Constitution provides the means and the proper locus through which encroachments between the three branches of power may be examined and settled.[120] However, the IO activities described throughout this Essay may also be conducted by most 21st century military superpowers. *A propos* the messianic rise of China, Henry Kissinger issued the following warning:

> Once China becomes strong enough to stand alone, it might discard us. A little later it might even turn against us, if its perception of its interests requires it.[121]

Much earlier, Napoléon Bonaparte predicted, "When China awakes, it will shake the world."[122] As such, case studies based on other countries' systems would be a welcome addition to research and analysis in this area.

Second, this Essay does not describe proposed IW legislation or military orders, but simply makes the theoretical case for preferring a domestic law approach to IW. Here, too, further research and analysis could be very fruitful.

Third, as the author acknowledges, the situation he proposes is not beyond debate. The proposed domestic law paradigm has its imperfections and limitations, as Table III summarizes below:

TABLE III. IMPERFECTIONS OF THE DOMESTIC LAW PARADIGM

1. Judicial and juridical challenges may be made if state statutes eventually also become Treaty Law.
2. Objections may be made to a "one-size-can-fit-all" approach, and the nexus to Jenks's common law approach may be challenged.
3. The lack of scientific and legal expertise on the part of individual Member States to analyze "high-tech" weapon systems may make it difficult for those states to develop domestic law regarding IW.
4. There is currently no clear international mandate or diplomatic support to sustain the eventual transition from domestic into international law.

In the end, however, despite these limitations, this Essay makes a strong case in favor of a domestic law approach to IW. Surely, such an approach would be better than the current alternative: an anarchic state that puts combatants and non-combatants alike at risk. It would also be superior to an international law approach that would likely lack enforceability and face very significant delay and opposition.

This Essay did not cover some of IW's most controversial areas of interest. In particular, details of IW's lethal information technologies and tactics, as well as some implications for existing space laws, should be explored. Further research should also encompass doctrinal and jurisprudential perspectives on the use of computers and computer systems as means or "instruments" of war. Moreover, there is a need for non-military institutions to start looking into the applicability of U.S. criminal statutes to IO, as well as some of the limitations of foreign criminal statutes *vis-à-vis* U.S. cyber warriors. Lastly, research should explore the question whether IW's premature and ill-conceived *modus operandi* may be unconstitutional.

ENDNOTES-V

[120]   *Id.* at 1259; *see also* Marbury *v.* Madison, *supra* note 27, at 163.

[121]   *See* Henry Kissinger, White House Years 1091(1979). Regarding a potentially dormant Russia, *see* Zhu Xiaoli & Zhao Xiaozhuo, Mei'E xin junshi geming (The United States and Russia in the New Military Revolution) (1996); *see also* the work of Timothy Thomas, *Testimony of Timothy Thomas, (Lt. Col., retired), Foreign Military Studies Office, U.S. Army Before the US-China Commission* (Aug. 3, 2001), *available at* http://www.uscc.gov/textonly/transcriptstx/testho.htm (last visited Nov. 28, 2008).

[122]   *See* Richard Bernstein & Ross Munro, The Coming Conflict With China 203 (1997)(noting the prescient call by Napoléon Bonaparte, vis-à-vis China).

VI. Outcomes of the Author's Prior Foresight Analyses

As Professor Tribe suggested earlier, the adoption of new technologies on the "battlefield" should be done with the utmost respect for the rule of law. Obama's timely call for a public debate over the Pentagon's cyber warfare program signals that credibility, diversity, and acceptance will require more than the common claim of "military necessity." For instance, as reported by Lolita Baldor of the Associated Press, the National Research Council, an independent group commissioned by the Obama Administration, concluded in 2009 that the government's policies on how and when to wage cyber warfare are ill-formed, lack adequate oversight, and require a broad public debate.[123]

In a piece submitted on March 30, 2009 to the Harvard Journal of Law & Technology (JOTL), the author had already declared:

[A] need for non-military institutions to
start looking into the applicability of U.S.
criminal statutes to IO, as well as some of
the limitations of foreign criminal statutes
vis-à-vis U.S. cyber warriors.[124]

The author reached similar conclusions going
back to the 2007 report (*Initial Supports to
Regulate Information Warfare's Potentially
Lethal Technologies and Techniques*), presented
at the Peter Kiewit Institute of the University
of Nebraska during the 3rd International
Conference on Information Warfare and
Security:

Lessons learned from the successful
establishment of previous international
instruments (Biological Warfare Convention
1972; Chemical Warfare Convention 1993)
suggest that, very restricted programs ran by
a few military schools lack the legitimacy and
diversity required to prepare the doctrinal
landscape for an international convention on
information warfare's most lethal weapons.
Although many foreign military programs
have been designed to keep track of this
fluid situation, military constraints do not
allow the same level of engagement afforded
by non-military scholars (whose positions

do not necessarily or officially engage their governments). Hence, until a very broad international consensus is reached, it would be premature (and even dangerous) to assume that lethal information warfare weapons (not specifically prohibited) are tacitly permitted.[125]

Based on the foregoing statements, Obama's call is an interesting turn of events vindicating the author's hard-fought-for and long-standing position. Moreover, Lt. Gen. Keith Alexander, the Pentagon's leading cyber warfare commander, recently acknowledged the United States' determination to use computer technology to deter or defeat enemies, while still protecting the public's constitutional rights. This acknowledgement indicates that there may be hope for bring all IW conducts and weapons within the boundaries of the rule of law. Coming from a top Pentagon official, Lt. Gen. Alexander's statement, in many aspects, marks a positive step towards protecting cyber warriors against potential charges of having committed IW war crimes and/or IW crimes against humanity.

As the title suggests, the author's prescient advice to Israel and others operating in the Middle East, through the piece *"Warning to Information Operations Planners: 'Ignore the Information Seeking Patterns of Potential Victims of Information Warfare in the Middle East at Your Peril,'"* submitted to the 5th Conference on i-Warfare and Security in 2008, could not have been more explicit:

> It has become a foremost priority for any IO planner to thoroughly analyze the impact of their operations on potential victims. It is more so for Middle Eastern countries, in which religion plays a primordial role . . . Of course, "low density Internet connections and lower volume of news outlets do not amount to IW immunity."[126]

Indeed, as the author warned a year earlier, the 2009 Israeli's assault on Gaza, after years of Palestinian rocket attacks, was met with web-enabled cell phones --broadcasting dramatic images around the world, despite a "record low volume of news outlets" on the ground. "IW immunity" did not materialize. As a result, humanitarian concerns contributed to an untimely Israeli pullout, followed by allegations of war crimes and crimes against humanity on both sides.[127]

With regard to the European anti-missile shield program, a perfect example of offensive/ defensive IO component, the author issued this prescient warning, during the Nebraska security conference and prior to the 2008 Caucasus conflict, in the following terms:

> Russia's possible response to the aforesaid "shield" is likely to involve new weapons and the triangular deterrence option: Russia, Iran, and Cuba (the RIC triangle). In other words, *Russia might feel the pressure to create new forward bases and very "dangerous liaisons" to deter what it perceives as a threat.* Considering on-going investigations into the infamous "waterboarding" scandal, allegations of torture, and Iran's undeniable rise in the Middle East, the U.S. is becoming more and more vulnerable on many fronts.[128]

Once again, following what he described as a "consultation" with his Defense Secretary and others, Obama scrapped the Bush-era futile shield — vindicating the author's two-year-old prediction that the multifaceted dimension of America's vulnerability would force its leaders into concessions over the issue. In fact, as the heat intensified during the

month of May 2009, Defense Secretary Robert
Gates went on a delicate mission, seeking to
reassure long-term U.S. allies in the Persian
Gulf region that efforts by Washington to
reach out to Iran will not come at their
expense.[129]

Further, when the Secretary of State
Condoleezza Rice played on Ukraine and
Poland's "innocence" — over a shield
program that was predestined to fail, as any
attentive expert on Russia should realize in
the post-911 context — the author's rebuttal
was lucid. It confirmed that, as of October
2008, the author had already qualified
the manufactured hype over the soon-to-be
scrapped shield as an "alibi." His report
forwarded to presidential candidate Barack
Obama via Prof. Bruce Aitken, a homeland
security expert very close to the Obama
campaign could not have been any clearer:

> In synthesis, irrespective of any alibi,
> even with the timely approval by Poland
> of the Missile Shield Agreement or renewed
> interests displayed by Ukraine and other
> former Soviet republics, the U.S. "show of
> force" came obviously several weeks too late
> in the Black Sea.[130]

Other passages from the same report also contained the following arguments and recommendations:

Recent events have triggered many warning signs pointing to an eventual challenge, by "Latin America," of the U.S. presence on Guantanamo Bay, under the claims of torture, crimes against humanity, war crimes, breach of contract, misuse of Cuban soil to engage in conducts that are deemed illegal by the U.S. highest Court and condemned by every living soul, but the Bush Administration . . .

The current momentum is clearly moving against America. The possibility of striking a miraculous deal with Latin America, despite the inescapable Guantanamo showdown, should not be ignored. However, as a result of any such deal, the Russia-Ukraine lease dispute runs the risk of being translated into a major blow against NATO and U.S. interests in Europe . . .

Guantanamo remains a wild card in a series of challenges that the Obama [Administration] will have to be careful in handling. Closing the prison will not put an end to the challenges ahead. I would even recommend that negotiations [be] held in parallel or prior to closing prison officially. In [other] words, this [is] one of many reasons why the United States will have to engage in direct talk with Cuba. We must keep in mind that Venezuela and other parties will have to be considered (by proxy), when proposing any deal.[131]

Some of the news headlines that followed the author's report were intriguing enough to capture worldwide attention, starting with these fiery lines from Cuban President Fidel Castro:

Maintaining a military base in Cuba against the will of the people violates the most elemental principles of international law.[132]

Thursday, January 29, 2009 10:41 PM EST: *Fidel Castro Demands Obama Return Guantanamo Base.*[133]

Thursday, January 29, 2009 22:43:50 GMT: *Chavez to US: Give Gitmo Back to Cuba.*[134]

Friday, January 30, 2009: *Castro Urges Guantanamo Bay Return.* [135]

Friday, May 1, 2009: *Clinton Warns of Iranian, Chinese, gains in Latin America.*[136]

Monday, May 4, 2009: *Congress Leery about Obama's Plan on tax Loopholes.*[137]

The author's foresight analyses did not always please everyone. He is often threatened by incompetent zealots in the name of national security. Undeterred, he remains an independent investigator and an assiduous advocate for long-lasting peace and security among nations. Accordingly, the following events are worth reporting:

When the author alerted U.S. authorities on the imminence of liquid explosives and other bioactive threats inside aircrafts and other confined spaces, "the focus," as he was told, "was on 'hard explosives' and 'pipe' bombs." Though he understood why U.S. authorities would focus their priorities elsewhere, basic findings from his doctoral research, during the (2004-2005) academic year, suggested that "cyber-conditioned terrorists" managed to mutate, hybridize, diversify, and adjust their methods to circumvent security measures widely politicized at the time. And when suspicion arose regarding political motives, analysts involved were routinely quieted by government officials. In fact, former Secretary of Homeland Security Tom Ridge recently conceded that he "was pressured to raise the terror alert to help Bush win re-election in 2004."[138]

As a result, to document the "cold shoulder" incident, the author filed a patent with the United States Patent Office on possible countermeasures.[139] He later relayed his concerns to Rep. Philip Brutus of Miami who promptly contacted and notified Sherriff Hunter of Broward County in early 2006. The author then flew to Finland, following what turned out to be a symbolic quick stop in London, for a major international security conference in Helsinki during which he also exposed the liquid explosive threat. Several members of the U.S. Secret Service and the U.S. Naval Criminal Investigative Service (USNCIS) attended the Helsinki conference. The audience also included British, Canadian, Russian, and other international defense and security officials. What the FBI did — or did not do — with the information might remain an intelligence matter dealing with sources and methods. However, there is no secret with regard to the outcome soon thereafter: British officials thwarted the "liquid explosive plot" targeting a series of intercontinental flights from London to locations across Canada and the United States on August 10, 2006.[140] At one point, endless lines at major airport hubs followed the ritual of emptying shampoo bottles and other common liquid containers. Separately, traces of polonium found inside of several aircrafts during the same period did not simplify matters.

Moreover, the most recent terrorist attack on the Saudi Prince Mohammed bin Nayef, head of Saudi Arabia's counterterrorism efforts, exemplifies the type of hybridization the author warned about. The attack involved a bomb hidden in the assailant's undergarment, in the vicinity of his rectum, and reportedly detonated by a chemical fuse to circumvent existing security measures: revealing the sophistication level of this new breed of cyber-conditioned terrorists. The July 2005 archives of Sharon Fain and David Lewkowict (Fox News) as well as reports and briefings filed with the FBI offices in Atlanta during the same period, according to retired FBI Special Agent Harold Copus, should reveal how much U.S. authorities had already learned — or failed — to learn about this specific type of attack.

From the very beginning, the author's notification, addressed to the FBI and dated October 17, 2003 carried the opening lines:

Enclosed is a brief write-up on the "Theory of Virtual Intelligence" prepared by Mr. Hyacinthe for his doctoral studies. This covers, in part, his theory to predict the national security requirements of the nation in 40 to 50 years. I am advising you of Mr. Hyacinthe's course of studies so that it does not trigger adverse responses by the Federal security departments. His request for information may result in unwarranted investigations.[141]

Indeed, America is slowly reckoning with a series of national security challenges that had been overlooked or simply ignored for too long. From a lack of imagination (as indicated in the 9/11 Commission Report) to unwarranted persecutions and borderline legal policies and practices, many ill-conceived decisions had to be reversed by the Obama Administration in order to comply with the rule of law and change his predecessor's perilous course of unilateralism. In the intelligence business, as it is often said, a little imagination can go a long way.

ENDNOTES-VI

[123] Lolita Baldor, *Report: Cyber Warfare Policies Lack Oversight*, (ASSOCIATED PRESS), *available at* http://www.msnbc.msn.com/id/30482502/ (last visited Sep. 26, 2009)(reporting National Research Council says U.S. policies require a broad public debate).

[124] Berg P. Hyacinthe, *The Juridical Notion of Information Warfare: Genesis of a Domestic Paradigm* (unpublished submission to HARV. J.L. & TECH. 1, 23, 33-34(2009)).

[125] Hyacinthe & Fleurantin, *supra* note 40, at 204.

[126] *See* Berg P. Hyacinthe, *supra* note 51 (warning cyber warriors against war crimes and crimes against humanity); *see also U.N. Probe Blames Israel for Deaths During Gaza Offensive* (CNN, May 6, 2009), *available at* http://edition. cnn.com/2009/WORLD/meast/05/06/un.israel. gaza/index.html (last visited Sept. 28, 2009) (reporting U.N. committee holding the Israeli government responsible for deaths and more than $10 million in damage to U.N. buildings during the recent military offensive in Gaza). *See also Palestinians call for Israel to be 'punished' for Gaza offensive*, (CNN NEWS, Sept. 29, 2009), *available at* http://edition.cnn.

com/2009/WORLD/meast/09/29/un.gaza.report/
index.html(last visited Sept. 29, 2009)
(renewing push to punish Israel for war
crimes).

[127] *Israel, Palestinians Cited for War Crimes*,
(Cbs News, Sep. 15, 2009), *available at* http://
www.cbsnews.com/stories/2009/09/15/world/
main5312943.shtml (last visited Sept. 28,
2009)(reporting on the U.N. probe led by
former South African judge Richard Goldstone,
who is Jewish and has strong ties to Israel:
"Israel committed actions amounting to war
crimes, possibly crimes against humanity,"
during its Dec. 27–Jan. 18 military operations
against Palestinian rocket squads in the
Gaza Strip. Similarly, the 575-page report
found evidence that "Palestinian armed groups
committed war crimes, as well as possibly
crimes against humanity" during the deadly
conflict); *See also Gaza Acts Amounted to
War Crimes, U.N. Report Says,* (Cnn.com Int'l,
Sept. 15), *available at* http://edition.cnn.
com/2009/WORLD/meast/09/15/un.gaza.incursion/
index.html (last visited Sept. 28, 2009)
(confirming widely reporting of the war crimes
allegations — also discussed in the New York
Times, Washington Post, BBC News, and other news
outlets).

[128]   Hyacinthe & Fleurantin, *supra* note 40, at
         209; *see also Thursday Meeting With Iran
         to Test Obama 'Engagement' Policy*, (CNN.COM,
         Sept. 30, 2009), available at http://edition.
         cnn.com/2009/POLITICS/09/29/us.iran/index.
         html(last visited Sept. 30, 2009)(marking
         Obama's shift from his predecessor's failed
         isolation policy).

[129]   Lara Jakes, *Gates to Reassure Gulf on Outreach
         to Iran*, ASSOCIATED PRESS, *available at* http://
         www. News.yahoo.com/s/ap/20090504/ap_on_go_
         ca_st_pe/ml_gates_mideast/print (last visited
         May 4, 2009)(reporting on Secretary Gates's
         expectation: an initial "closed fist" from
         Iran). With Russia's constant pressure to
         regain its superpower status, maintaining
         its relationship with Iran, while reassuring
         others (e.g., Venezuela and Cuba), will set
         concessions with U.S. and Israel on — as the
         expression so conveniently fits — Russian
         roulettes. Many intelligence analysts doubted
         that Cuba would ever get over its Russian
         deception during the "so-called" Cuban missile
         crisis. However, Cuba seems to be moving
         beyond old grudges in a very timely manner to
         punish its enemies. Now, the pressure is very
         high on Russia: the Iranian crisis is likely
         to turn into a Russian showdown with Russia

holding all the cards in its hands — from its close relationship with China to its energy pipelines "feeding" major European countries and the aforementioned RIC triangle, stretching simultaneously across Latin America and the Middle East.

[130] Report prepared during October and November 2008 and forwarded to Barack Obama via Prof. Bruce Aitken, former professor at Georgetown Law School and American University Law School in Washington, DC. Of course, the report was made available to the author's academic advisors. A copy of the report was later forwarded to CNN analyst Roland S. Martin.

[131] See Id; see also Senior U.S. Official Holds Talks in Cuba, (CNN.COM, Sept. 30, 2009), available at http://edition.cnn.com/2009/ WORLD/americas/09/29/us.cuba.talks/index. html(last visited, Oct. 2, 2009)(reporting on a meeting between U.S. Acting Deputy Assistant Secretary Bisa Williams and Cuban Deputy Foreign Minister Dagoberto Rodriguez to restore mail service).

[132] Fidel Castro Demands Obama Return Guantanamo Base, (REUTERS, Jan. 29, 2009) available at www. reuters.com/articlePrint?articlId=USN2928671 9 (last visited Jan. 29, 2009)(reporting on ailing Cuban leader Fidel Castro's demand).

133   *Id.*(Castro, who has recently praised Obama
       as "honest" and "noble," lashed out at his
       administration for stating that Washington
       will not return Guantanamo if it has any
       military use for the United States and without
       concessions in return).

134   *Chavez to US: Give Gitmo Back to Cuba,* (PRESS TV,
       Jan. 29, 2009), *available at* http://www. Presstv.
       com/pop/print.aspx?id=84083 (last visited
       Jan. 29, 2009)(Venezuelan leader Hugo Chavez
       has urged US President Barack Obama to return
       the military base of Guantanamo to Cuba after
       applauding his decision to close the center).

135   *Castro Urges Guantanamo Bay Return,* (MSN
       NEWS, Jan. 30, 2009), *available at* http://
       www. News.uk.msn.com/world/article.aspx?cp-
       documentid=13478279 (last visited Jan. 30,
       2009) (announcing that Mr. Obama has ordered
       the prison for terror suspects on the U.S.
       base to be closed within a year, but Cuba
       also demands the return of the 45-square mile
       territory the base occupies in the island's
       east). Surprisingly, Obama was fiercely
       criticized for his lack of a post-closure
       action plan. He consequently paid a heavy
       political price and signaled a failure to meet
       his self-imposed deadline. Did Obama receive
       the author's report? Did his advisors ignore

it? Only Prof. Aitken and the President's entourage can answer these questions.

136   *Clinton Warns of Iranian, Chinese, Gains in Latin America* (CNN NEWS, MAY 1, 2009; courtesy of Charley Keyes, CNN Senior Producer, from a town hall meeting at the State Department with senior Foreign Service Officers during the month of May, 2009), *available at* http://www. edition.cnn.com/2009/POLITICS/05/01/clinton. latin.america/index.html)(last visited May 1, 2009)(reporting Secretary of State Hillary Clinton saying: U.S. having to counter efforts by China, Russia, and Iran in [the]region). The Secretary of State specifically noted, "If you look at the gains, particularly in Latin America, that Iran is making and China is making, it is quite disturbing." Dangerous "liaisons" or "quite disturbing" gains? In both cases, the reasoning displays striking similarities.

137   *Congress Leery about Obama's Plan on tax Loopholes,* (ASSOCIATED PRESS, May 4, 2009), *available at http://www.news.yahoo.com/s/ ap/20090504/ap_on_go_pr_wh_/us_obama_taxes/ print* (last visited May 4, 2009) (reporting on President Barack Obama's stern promise to crack down on companies "that ship jobs overseas" and move "jobs off our shores or transferring

profits to overseas tax heavens."). Moreover, welcoming Obama's statements, Rep. Charles Rangel, chairman of the tax-writing House Ways and Means Committees has this much to say: "For too long, our tax laws have rewarded companies that invest and keep their money overseas and turned a blind eye to the use of tax havens by the wealthy."

138 *See*, TOM RIDGE & LARRY BLOOM, THE TEST OF OUR TIMES: AMERICA UNDER SIEGE (2009).

139 Hyacinthe, *supra* note 51 (targeting bioactive threats inside aircrafts on July 19, 2005 — with Figure 7 very specifically showing an aircraft under attack).

140 *Q&A: Liquid Explosives*, (BBC, Aug. 10, 2006), *available at* http://news.bbc.co.uk/2/hi/science/nature/4780391.stm(last viewed Sept. 29, 2009) (reporting on Scotland Yard's revelation of an alleged terror plot to blow up planes from the UK mid-flight and cause mass murderer on an unimaginable scale).

However, very little had been reported, thus far, on how U.S. officials reportedly hampered British evidence-gathering in this "liquid explosives" case. For example, the involvement of suspected plotter Rashid Rauf is worth revisiting. According to Andy Hayman, the Metropolitan Police's assistant commissioner for special operations at the time of the plot, the Bush White House panicked as British officials reported mounting evidence of a plan to target U.S. cities: "We believed the Americans had demanded [Rauf's] arrest and we were angry we had not been informed," Hayman told The London Times. "The arrest hampered our evidence-gathering and placed us in Britain under intolerable pressure" he complained.

Though liquid explosives occupied the forefront, the UK had been unsuccessfully pressing Pakistan for Rauf's extradition over the 2002 murder of his uncle. Further, Rauf was reportedly involved in the decapitation of American journalist Daniel Pearl. Furthermore, Rauf was connected through many "nodes" with the Jaish-e-Mohammed — a banned group that had earlier become one of the most powerful armed Islamist organizations involved in attacks against India over the disputed region of Kashmir. See also Profile: Rashid Rauf, (BBC News, Nov. 22, 2008), available at http://news.bbc.co.uk/2/hi/uk_news/7743339. stm (last visited Sept. 27, 2009)(providing more details on Rauf, son of a successful UK businessman, as one of the alleged "liquid explosives" plotters). As Rauf's profile,

Hayman's account, and the author's own report suggest, this "liquid explosives" plot remains a bizarre episode involving Pakistani, U.S., and UK intelligence agencies.

The polonium incident, involving a former Russian spy, got even murkier in London. Nonetheless, in both cases, "bioactive substances inside aircrafts and other confined spaces" threatened innocent civilians — irrespective of nationality, race, or religious beliefs (see the author's U.S. patent application number 60/700,700,708 filed in 2005 against these threats) still experiencing unreasonable delay at the time of redaction of this Essay).

[141] Notification sent to the FBI through author's counsel on October 17, 2003, while attending Florida State University in Tallahassee, Florida.

VII. CONCLUSION

In closing, as a melting pot, America is the experimental laboratory wherein periodically "good" is contrasted with "evil" so that lessons learned may, to a large extent, benefit mankind. But nonetheless, compliance with the rule of law must remain invariable.

The American system is assumed to be very committed to the rule of law. As a result, unfortunate circumstances, often attended by incompetent and/or corrupt officials who incongruously endanger U.S. national security in the name of national security, tend to steer the country into a legal conundrum.

Lessons learned from recent international conflicts suggest that the world can be a better place with an America that promotes inventiveness, while abiding by the rule of law. Though the American system has never been perfect, recent challenges to America's moral authority have sent concerned citizens and true patriots back to the drawing board. The thirst for a new political current and a fresh stream of "error-correct" policies had been overwhelmingly manifested all throughout Barack Obama's successful campaign.

Today, President Obama calls for much needed "smart power" to counter emergent threats against the United States. And given the priority accorded to IW by the U.S. military, good legal advice is needed before venturing any further. Smart power is a multifaceted secret weapon revealed, *infra*, through the equation: Smart Power = Rule of Law ÷ Citizen Inventiveness.

On the spirit of innovation, "it is only by building a new foundation that we will once again harness that incredible generative capacity of the American people" the President said, during his weekly address to the nation on August 1, 2009. "All it takes are the policies to tap that potential — to ignite that spark of creativity and ingenuity — which has always been at the heart of who we are and how we succeed."

The establishment of a juridical notion of IW might be a good starting point, for the ultimate power to control/distribute emerging digital information technologies — including the most advanced military technologies — will rest, not with inventors and manufacturers of the latest gadget, but with the most credible regulatory body. The latter would have acquired, a priori, the appropriate level of legal IW expertise. Of course, "information dominance" has taken new meanings.

However, short of an established juridical notion of IW, it is very difficult to imagine any credible claims of legal IW expertise. The current military "monopoly" over the issue does not help the situation, for a broader, more diverse academic setting is required in order to encompass depth and breadth, and to establish suitable definitions for IW conducts, IW damages, and IW responsibilities.

It has been widely reported that IW activities are neither illegal nor legal under international law. The popularity of such ambivalent paradigm calls for caution. In practice, U.S. domestic statutes, effectively checked through congressional oversight, do not seem to be as lenient. As the recent CIA "clash" with Congress (on and about June 23, 2009) over yet another borderline legal Bush-era program suggests, even covert operations — often labeled as "sting operations" by the FBI — conducted on U.S. soil or abroad, require legal backing. Therefore, it is hard to imagine a scenario wherein Congress

would waive its constitutional oversight
duties by allowing unchecked cyber warriors to
engage in unrestricted IW activities.[142] With
or without digital information technologies,
official declaration of war rests "primarily"
with Congress. The few exceptions allowed to
the Commander-in-Chief still require prompt
and timely (post-deployment) reporting to
Congress, as established by statutes above.

Any "smart" superpower should favor
explicit IW regulations, for the development
of the direct ascent ASAT system and its
potential proliferation, for example, will
target space-based military might at its core:
spacecrafts and communications satellites.
Unfortunately, the proliferation of space
technologies is likely to amplify the nuclear
threat in the near future. As such, of course,
outer-space reach by U.S. rivals calls for
interstellar concerns. Privately, military
planners are still struggling to deal with
the new reality: a non-sovereign territory
(e.g., space and outer-space) was not the best
and safest location to anchor a strategic
Command-and-Control IO outpost. Article 2 of
the 1967 Outer Space Treaty very specifically
holds that "Outer space, including the moon
and other celestial bodies, is not subject

to national appropriation" by any means, not only including formal claims of sovereignty, but use or occupation as well. Further, the treaty opened these bodies to "use by all States without discrimination of any kind, on a basis of equality" with all enjoying "free access to all areas."

There is a legitimate fear concerning the growing number of nations aspiring to space power. However, as the evidence shows, there are very limited legal options available against these nations' aspiration: the rule of law and existing international treaties and conventions are on their side. The question remains: Can these emergent powers live up to expectations? Irrespective of any answer to this question, continuing dissuasive attempts by established superpowers are likely to be hampered — given the potential impact a forthcoming "modified map" of the international community's geopolitical landscape will entail.

America's early dominance over the high-tech market could not withstand Asia's aggressive technological expansion, at a time when mismanaged wars in Iraq and Afghanistan coincided with "corporate greed" to shake the foundation of the entire American system.

The dilemma is not as simple as it seems: the crisis was economic — e.g., involving product, price, and place, rather than financial in nature. China, India, Japan, and other emergent economic powers are producing electronics goods America expected to sell to others. Latin America is leaning to the left, while the Caribbean islands' buying power continues to plummet. France, Germany, Great Britain, and Russia lead the European markets. Widespread anti-American sentiment in the Middle East intertwines with what many African nations perceive as a deliberate and rancorous "American abandonment," to complicate America's current struggle. Meanwhile, new and more competitive players are gaining access to these lucrative markets. Can America rely solely on its domestic consumers for a full and lasting recovery?

Charles M. Vest, then-President of the Massachusetts Institute of Technology (MIT), warned, back in January, 1996:

> Every rapidly developing nation in the world is banking on technology to move it into competitiveness on the world stage. The U.S. cannot afford to lose its edge and our region most of all cannot afford to have this happen.[143]

Given the unfolding consequences of the Guantanamo debacle, it is in America's best interest to reverse its defunct foreign policy stand *vis-à-vis* Latin America and the Caribbean islands. Henceforth, America's success in other parts of the world will weigh heavily on its handling of this Guantanamo chapter, and on how it responds to the new challenge in Latin America and the Caribbean islands. America should not repeat its miscalculation with respect to the influence of Brazil, Venezuela, Cuba and their allies in the region. The Guantanamo saga has caused irreparable damages to America's image and its ability to negotiate on several critical international dossiers (from Latin America to Eastern Europe and the Middle East).

Though often portrayed otherwise by many analysts within the intelligence community, Guantanamo remains a hidden national security liability to the United States. Reigning on "lawless lands" is widely recognized as a Taliban trademark. America can and should do better: there is always another way, always. Returning Guantanamo to Cuba involves a complicated transaction undoubtedly beyond the scope of this Essay; but applying the rule of law to detainees held in the Guantanamo

Bay prison system in Cuba is expressly the type of action promoted here — for doing otherwise would constitute a danger to the national security of the United Sates.

The most credible threats against U.S. national security can easily be debunked according to the following quintet:

1. Mastery of propaganda and manipulation of public opinion by the enemy (e.g., psychological IW using Web services and other media outlets).

2. Reinvention of guerilla warfare and "flavored" insurgencies to adjust to shock and awe — a deadly formula against the revolution in military affairs' paradigm, for more boots, not less, will be required to fight under these conditions.

3. Interplanetary weapons targeting communication satellites and other air/spacecrafts — as the direct ascent ASAT system tests suggest. Unruly cyber warriors would fall under this category.

4. Demonizing Barack Husein Obama as an alien American whose citizenship is still being challenged in U.S. courts. The American people expect a proud American Obama to negotiate with Russia, China, Iran, Iraq, Pakistan, Afghanistan, Cuba, North Korea,

Venezuela, and others — on a series of fiddly national security *dossiers* previously mishandled by incompetent/ corrupt officials. Meanwhile, his own countrymen continue to rebuke him as a "fake" U.S. citizen. How much respect will Obama lose from foreign observers and other world leaders? How much will his ability to negotiate with foreign governments on national security matters be affected by these malicious attacks/insults? Sadly, many signs point to a situation where U.S. national security is being traded against 2010 electoral ambitions, even if it means to insult the President of the United States during a Joint Session of Congress speech to an audience of 32.1 million viewers, or deliberately provoking other African-Americans in the hope of fueling a race debate from which the President has been trying so hard to recoil.

5. The hybrid threat combining a series of scattered "hotspots" around the world with a well-coordinated "coalition of the unwilling" to challenge, or perhaps to overwhelm, the adversarial alliance commonly dubbed as the "coalition of the willing." The scattered threat is tactical, while the

alliance-based threat is strategic. It is worth noting that terrorism and WMD threats are likely to manifest in transmutation within the aforesaid quintet.

The abovementioned foreign policy challenges should serve as an astounding reminder: as America moves forward with the implementation of its strategic IW master plan, it should not settle for an "extrajudicial" short-term homeland security compromise, which will later translate into long-term national security threats.

Lately, with a fortunate emphasis on creativity and ingenuity, significant efforts have been deployed to ensure that U.S. national security is "rethought" and "reframed" within the boundaries of the rule of law — to reflect new realities. It is encouraging to watch America reinventing and renewing itself. However, it is still very tempting for Obama Administration officials to resort to scare tactics based on the following reasons:

1. The "spectacle-hungry" crowd continues to yearn for more flashy arrests linking terrorist suspects to — for some odd reasons, unnamed — "top Al Qaida leaders"

and for spectacular news conferences featuring Bush-era drumbeats of fear such as "most serious terrorist threat since 9/11."

2. The major players who fueled the previous administration's "gospel of fear" are still serving in high-ranking law enforcement and intelligence positions today.

As part of his agenda to revitalize a recently 'duped,' but courageous American people, and for the sake of his own legacy, Obama might want to rebuke and reject such tactics. He can achieve superior results reverting back to his silence and effective 'non-media-driven' strategy that led to the elimination of (real, identified, and notorious) terrorist leaders throughout Pakistan, Afghanistan, Indonesia, Somalia, and the Philippines within a record timeframe: marking a real difference between "claiming" national security and "availing" it; "claiming" country first and veritably "putting" it first. Thus, with the serial decapitation of these enigmatic foreign figures and mentors, the so-called homegrown terrorists —not to be confused with cases where federal agents utilize "techno entrapment" to settle old scores — are likely to be reduced to predictable "planners," with very little chance to succeed on U.S. soil: unable to materialize their threats through triumphant attacks. But there is problem: a successful infiltration of the Obama camp by powerful rivals who "want him to fail" can be disastrous in this context.

History is likely to reveal — as done in other top secret "slaps" to the U.S. Constitution: Vietnam, Watergate, Iran-Contra, Abu Dhabi, and Guantanamo, to avoid an exhaustive list — that Obama might have been constrained, in very peculiar ways, to retain a cadre of perfidious officials in top positions in his administration. And going one step further, unless a pretrial agreement is reached in favor of the former Illinois Governor, *United States v. Rod R. Blagojevich & John Harris* is likely to bring up — if not bring in — several "powerful players" from both sides of the American political spectrum for an unprecedented showdown in Chicago: auguring an inescapable exhumation of the scandal surrounding Obama's Illinois seat. Will "Senategate" measure up to Watergate?

On the "most serious threat since 9/11" rhetoric, there is hardly enough evidence to support such a claim, for the underlying mechanism that generates the charge is not even evidential. As for the gratuitous and chronic reminder of a looming attack greater or equal in magnitude to the 9/11 carnage, from Al Qaida *et al.*, on U.S. soil, it is an amalgam of wishful thinking and post-9/11 psychological IW's rogue tactics in action. Evidently, former U.S. Secretary of Homeland Security Tom Ridge's above captured testimony confirmed that the American public had been injected repeatedly with very potent doses of this torturous psychological IW liturgy, for political reasons under the previous Administration: exemplifying the type of IW conduct that needs to be codified through new legislations promptly, so as to facilitate Information Age judicial proceedings.

In setting out to measure immaterialized and intangible threats against tangible and material damages sustained during the 9/11 attacks, the fear-mongers run the risk of being accused of having caused intentional psychological harms, knowingly and willfully, to the general public for political gain. These ill-minded believers in the "gospel of fear" tend to rely on convenient fuzzy statistics deliberately: mixing apples with oranges.

The fear-induced popularity of Obama's predecessor was ephemeral, and the end result was ruinous. Now, Obama has a clear decision to make, while the entire world is banking on his success — as the 2009 Nobel Peace Prize award suggests.

Some analysts continue to paint a "soft on defense and security" picture, while others proclaim an "end to the U.S. public's honeymoon with Obama." But the reality on the ground reveals an energizing spark of smart power. Beyond politics, national security requirements and strategic IW policies ought to be established in tandem. The emerging U.S. national security paradigm, discussed throughout this Essay, aims at the ubiquitous reach, the apogee of "smart power," from physical space to cyberspace and outer space, according to a new strategic IW mindset: Obama's national security agendum.

Indeed, with smart power come enormous cyber warrior responsibilities. For example, psychological warfare, espionage, economic intelligence, counterespionage, and military drone-related operations are contentious activities that would need to be handled guardedly under the current conditions. Notably, U.S. military drones have been "overexposed" in Afghanistan as well as in Pakistan. As a result, in addition to questions related to benefit-cost ratio, sources and methods are being compromised with respect to more able combatants and future conflicts. There has been a widespread, and unfortunate, acceptance by the American public of yet another myth — the myth that military drones are operating without heavy reliance on "eyes and ears" on the ground. In reality, contrary to the extraordinary autonomy projected through military propaganda and by profit-minded defense contractors, the efficiency of some of these drones comes with the ultimate sacrifice of human intelligence on the ground — e.g., brave servicemen, servicewomen, and gay personnel of the U.S. military *et al.*, infiltrating very dangerous organizations and forbidden enemy territories. In synthesis, any impartial analysis should account for the hidden human cost associated with these spectacular missile strikes, seemingly misrepresented as "human-risk-free." Humanitarian concerns have also been raised on both sides of this issue.

It is worth acknowledging that the U.S. military is currently operating its drones, in the tribal regions along Pakistan's border with Afghanistan, on safer legal grounds with "overt" endorsement from Pakistani officials. Under the previous regime of strikes, the U.S. did not claim responsibility, as several Pakistani officials publicly stated that these drone-related missile strikes violated their territorial sovereignty. Civilian casualties came up as another contentious issue during the debate.

However, given that the CIA may have obtained some form of "covert" *laissez-passer* from political and/or military Pakistani officials to comply with international laws (e.g., dealing with the sovereignty issue, prior to initial strikes), legal analysts need to proceed with prudence. As a 99% clandestine agency, the CIA is not under any obligations to comment publicly on on-going sensitive operations, though the rule of law must always prevail according to statutory reporting requirements and congressional oversight outlined in the National Security Act of 1947.

From sunshine laws to freedom of information acts and international human rights legislations

(e.g., Sweden's Freedom of the Press Act of
1772; Article 19 of the Universal Declaration
of Human Rights of 1948; and America's Bill of
Rights of 1971), the general public is legally
entitled to fair and balanced reporting on
major military operations likely to cause mass
casualties, to produce extensive damages,
and/or to result in enormous economic harms.
Some of these provisions expressly protect
prudent auditors/reporters against government
retaliation.[144] As such, it is important to
note the carefully drafted language — e.g.,
"may have," "potentially," and "might have"
violated international laws — used by most
legal scholars, when discussing military and/
or intelligence matters.

Cyber warriors remain at war — at war
with the constraining dicta of the rule of
law (e.g., dealing with separation of powers
and congressional oversight); at war to
protect the "homeland" against the ominous
threats of cyber-conditioned terrorists
and "non-state" actors (e.g., protecting
critical infrastructures and engaging in
"unprecedented" computer-assisted covert
operations); and at war against state-
sponsored hackers and hostile cyber warriors

(e.g., fighting against very capable rivals and enemies via strategic IW).

Lastly, as dependence on telecommunications systems to operate more sophisticated military drones intensifies, U.S. national security will get more intertwined with space security and the laws that govern IW technologies and techniques. Beyond legitimate legal concerns ranging from violation of territorial integrity of foreign nations to weaponization of space and outer-space, the involvement of cyber warriors, using military drones and other "novel" means to engage in direct combat, ignites a peculiar wave of "friendly fire" or self-inflicted psychological torture on the battlefield today:

> When you come in at 500-600 mph, drop a 500-pound bomb and then fly away, you don't see what happens. When a Predator fires a missile, you watch it all the way to impact, and I mean it's very vivid, it's right there and personal. So it does stay in people's minds for a long time.
>
> — Col. Albert K. Aimar, U.S. Air Force

ENDNOTES-VII

[142]   Hyacinthe *supra* note 51, at 27 (asserting that,
even where creative interpretations — defining
simple logic — had erroneously prevailed over
the rule of law, a "fuzzy" undeclared war
status, by its very nature, could not have been
knowingly authorized by the U.S. Congress).

[143]   *See MIT President Warns Economic Growth
is Threatened by Cuts,* (MIT, Jan. 22,
1996), *available at* http://web.mit.edu/
newsoffice/1996/econgrowth.html# (last visited
Oct. 7, 2009) (discussing the prospect of U.S.
losing its technological edge and signaling
a system in danger of being broken).

[144]   *See* Swedish Constitution; First Amendment
of the United States Constitution; United
Nations; *see* also Freedom of Information Acts
of 1997 and 2003.

VIII. Acknowledgements

Special thanks go to retired FBI Special Agent Harold Copus and Officer Francine Ware. I also want to thank James Mudd, Leo Ochs, and Skip Camp of Collier County Government for their initial support.

To Prof. Gathegi (my PhD advisor, Florida State University), Prof. Guglielmi (my LLD advisor, Assas School of Law, La Sorbonne), Prof. Burke, Prof. Liu, Prof. Lustria, Prof. Stuckey-French, Prof. Koubi, Mom, Dad, Titi, Sophie, Aramentha, Brunel, Dave*, Mimi, Kako, Ekna, and Elie, I will forever be grateful.

Separately, I should thank Zia Hayat of BAE Systems, UK, Dr. Boukhtouta of Defense Canada, Monsieur Goretta of France's Defense Department (DGA), and Dr. Popp of U.S. DARPA (Defense Research Program Agency) for their initial feedback on the annexed autonomous biochemical defense concept.

The credit belongs to many people within the international intelligence community who

will not be identified by name because of the
nature of what they do.

Artwork & Cover Page: Alain LAFOSSE/Fluidiax,
Paris, France.

Larry R. Fleurantin, Esq.
Renaud Hyppolite, Esq.

IX. Author's Recent Publications

Hyacinthe, B. (*in press*). Information Operations in Space, Absence of Space Sovereignty, Growing Number of Nations Looking Spaceward: Threats and Fears Concerning Established Space-based Military Powers, *5th International Conference on Information Warfare* and Security, *The Air Force Institute of Technology, Wright-Patterson Air Force Base, Ohio*.

Hyacinthe, B. (2009). Warning to Information Operations Planners: "Ignore the information seeking patterns of potential victims of Information Warfare in the Middle East at your peril," *5th Conference on i-Warfare and Security*, Cape Town. pp. 27-34.

Hyacinthe, B. and Fleurantin, L. (2008). Initial Supports to Regulate Information Warfare's Potentially Lethal Technologies and Techniques. *3rd International Conference on* *i-Warfare and Security*, Peter Kiewit Institute, University of Nebraska Omaha, USA. pp. 202-213.

Hyacinthe, B. (2007). *Users' adoption of emergent technologies: "Towards an acceptable model for safer cyber-assisted olfactory information exchanges in standard, micro, and nano systems."* Florida State University Electronic Theses and Dissertations System, Tallahassee, Florida, etd-07162007-171934.

Hyacinthe *et al.* (2007). Lethal Mutation versus Messianic Singularity: "A New Multidimensional Perspective on the Reciprocal Function of Digital Information Technologies as Offensive and Defensive Weapon Systems." *6th European Conference on Information Warfare and Security,* Defence Academy of the United Kingdom, Shrivenham, UK. pp. 99-108.

Hyacinthe, B. and Anglade, Y. (2007) "Conceptual Design of a Microfluidics Suppressor to Protect against Potentially Lethal Printing Devices: A Scenario-Based Physical Cyber Security Measure", *IC IW 2007: 2nd International Conference on i-Warfare and Security*, U.S. Naval Postgraduate School, Monterey, California. pp. 101-110.

Hyacinthe, B. (2006). Autonomous Biochemical Decontaminator (ABCD) against Weapons of Mass Destruction. *SPIE, vol. 6021:1-16*. Orlando, USA.

Hyacinthe, B. (2006). Hidden Global Security Threats and Emerging Technologies Exposed through Information Warfare Paradigms. *Proc. of the 5th European Conference on Information Warfare and Security*, Helsinki, Finland. pp. 101-110.

Hyacinthe, B. (2006). Methods and Apparatus for the Production of Aromatic and Gustatory Information. *JDCL*, Chapel Hill, NC. ACM 1-59593-354-9.

Patent Applications

Hyacinthe, B. (2006). Apparatus and Methods to Suppress Fluidic Diffusion of Unwanted Substances in Standard Systems, Nano-devices, and Bio-microelectromechanical Systems. *United States Patent and Trade Office*, VA. No. US-60/814320.

Hyacinthe, B. (2005). System and Device for Prevention and Neutralization of Bioactive Substances and Generating an Aroma-producing

Substance. *United States Patent and Trade Office*, VA. No. US-60/700,700,708.

Hyacinthe, B. (2005). Universal Cellular Circuit Board. *United States Patent and Trade Office*, VA. US-60/601658035.

Hyacinthe, B. (2004). Emergency Rescue Vehicle. United States Patent and Trade Office, VA. No. US60/634,637.

X. APPENDICES[**]

- Ten Years of UN Reactions
- Multifaceted Nature of The Cyber Warrior's Field of Intervention Illustrated

---

[**] *See* the United States Patent and Trade Office for full disclosure and explanation of figures.

General Assembly

Distr.
GENERAL

A/RES/53/70
4 January 1999

Fifty-third session
Agenda item 63

RESOLUTION ADOPTED BY THE GENERAL ASSEMBLY

[on the report of the First Committee (A/53/576)]

53/70.   Developments in the field of information and telecommunications in the context of international security

The General Assembly,

Recalling its resolutions on the role of science and technology in the context of international security, in which, *inter alia,* it recognized that scientific and technological developments could have both civilian and military applications and that progress in science and technology for civilian applications needed to be maintained and encouraged,

Noting that considerable progress has been achieved in developing and applying the latest information technologies and means of telecommunication,

Affirming that it sees in this process the broadest positive opportunities for the further development of civilization, the expansion of opportunities for cooperation for the common good of all States, the enhancement of the creative potential of mankind, and additional improvements in the circulation of information in the global community,

Recalling in this connection the approaches and principles outlined at the Information Society and Development Conference, held at Midrand, South Africa, from 13 to 15 May 1996,

Taking note of the results of the Ministerial Conference on Terrorism, held in Paris on 30 July 1996, and of the recommendations it made,[1]

---

[1] See A/51/261, annex.

99-76003

/...

Noting that the dissemination and use of information technologies and means affect the interests of the entire international community and that optimum effectiveness is enhanced by broad international cooperation,

Expressing concern that these technologies and means can potentially be used for purposes that are inconsistent with the objectives of maintaining international stability and security and may adversely affect the security of States,

Considering that it is necessary to prevent the misuse or exploitation of information resources or technologies for criminal or terrorist purposes,

1.   *Calls upon* Member States to promote at multilateral levels the consideration of existing and potential threats in the field of information security;

2.   *Invites* all Member States to inform the Secretary-General of their views and assessments on the following questions:

(*a*)   General appreciation of the issues of information security;

(*b*)   Definition of basic notions related to information security, including unauthorized interference with or misuse of information and telecommunications systems and information resources;

(*c*)   Advisability of developing international principles that would enhance the security of global information and telecommunications systems and help to combat information terrorism and criminality;

3.   *Requests* the Secretary-General to submit a report to the General Assembly at its fifty-fourth session;

4.   *Decides* to include in the provisional agenda of its fifty-fourth session an item entitled "Developments in the field of information and telecommunications in the context of international security".

79th plenary meeting
4 December 1998

UNITED
NATIONS

A

General Assembly

Distr.
GENERAL

A/RES/54/49
23 December 1999

Fifty-fourth session
Agenda item 71

RESOLUTION ADOPTED BY THE GENERAL ASSEMBLY

[*on the report of the First Committee (A/54/558)*]

54/49. Developments in the field of information and telecommunications in the context of international security

The General Assembly,

Recalling its resolution 53/70 of 4 December 1998,

Recalling also its resolutions on the role of science and technology in the context of international security, in which, *inter alia*, it recognized that scientific and technological developments could have both civilian and military applications and that progress in science and technology for civilian applications needed to be maintained and encouraged,

Noting that considerable progress has been achieved in developing and applying the latest information technologies and means of telecommunication,

Affirming that it sees in this process the broadest positive opportunities for the further development of civilization, the expansion of opportunities for cooperation for the common good of all States, the enhancement of the creative potential of mankind and additional improvements in the circulation of information in the global community,

Recalling in this connection the approaches and principles outlined at the Information Society and Development Conference, held at Midrand, South Africa, from 13 to 15 May 1996,

99-77713

/...

Taking note of the results of the Ministerial Conference on Terrorism, held in Paris on 30 July 1996, and of the recommendations it made,[1]

Noting that the dissemination and use of information technologies and means affect the interests of the entire international community and that optimum effectiveness is enhanced by broad international cooperation,

Expressing concern that these technologies and means can potentially be used for purposes that are inconsistent with the objectives of maintaining international stability and security and may adversely affect the security of States in both civilian and military fields,

Considering that it is necessary to prevent the misuse or exploitation of information resources or technologies for criminal or terrorist purposes,

Noting the contribution of those Member States that have submitted their assessments on issues of information security to the Secretary-General pursuant to paragraphs 1 to 3 of resolution 53/70,

Taking note of the report of the Secretary-General containing those assessments,[2]

Welcoming the timely initiative taken by the Secretariat and the United Nations Institute for Disarmament Research in convening an international meeting of experts at Geneva in August 1999 on developments in the field of information and telecommunications in the context of international security,

Considering that the assessments of Member States contained in the report of the Secretary-General and the international meeting of experts have contributed to a better understanding of the substance of issues of international information security, related notions and possible measures to limit the threats emerging in this field,

1.	*Calls upon* Member States to promote further at multilateral levels the consideration of existing and potential threats in the field of information security;

2.	*Invites* all Member States to continue to inform the Secretary-General of their views and assessments on the following questions:

(*a*)	General appreciation of the issues of information security;

(*b*)	Definition of basic notions related to information security, including unauthorized interference with or misuse of information and telecommunications systems and information resources;

(*c*)	Advisability of developing international principles that would enhance the security of global information and telecommunications systems and help to combat information terrorism and criminality;

---

[1] A/51/261, annex.

[2] A/54/213.

/...

3.   *Requests* the Secretary-General to submit a report to the General Assembly at its fifty-fifth session;

4.   *Decides* to include in the provisional agenda of its fifty-fifth session the item entitled "Developments in the field of information and telecommunications in the context of international security".

69th plenary meeting
1 December 1999

 **General Assembly**

Distr.: General
20 December 2000

Fifty-fifth session
Agenda item 68

Resolution adopted by the General Assembly

[on the report of the First Committee (A/55/554)]

55/28. Developments in the field of information and telecommunications in the context of international security

The General Assembly,

Recalling its resolutions 53/70 of 4 December 1998 and 54/49 of 1 December 1999,

Recalling also its resolutions on the role of science and technology in the context of international security, in which, inter alia, it recognized that scientific and technological developments could have both civilian and military applications and that progress in science and technology for civilian applications needed to be maintained and encouraged,

Noting that considerable progress has been achieved in developing and applying the latest information technologies and means of telecommunication,

Affirming that it sees in this process the broadest positive opportunities for the further development of civilization, the expansion of opportunities for cooperation for the common good of all States, the enhancement of the creative potential of mankind and additional improvements in the circulation of information in the global community,

Recalling in this connection the approaches and principles outlined at the Information Society and Development Conference, held at Midrand, South Africa, from 13 to 15 May 1996,

Bearing in mind the results of the Ministerial Conference on Terrorism, held in Paris on 30 July 1996, and the recommendations it made,[1]

Noting that the dissemination and use of information technologies and means affect the interests of the entire international community and that optimum effectiveness is enhanced by broad international cooperation,

Expressing concern that these technologies and means can potentially be used for purposes that are inconsistent with the objectives of maintaining international

---

[1] See A/51/261, annex.

00 56107

stability and security and may adversely affect the security of States in both civil and military fields,

Noting the contribution of those Member States that have submitted their assessments on issues of information security to the Secretary-General pursuant to paragraphs 1 to 3 of resolutions 53/70 and 54/49,

Taking note of the reports of the Secretary-General containing those assessments,[2]

Welcoming the initiative taken by the Secretariat and the United Nations Institute for Disarmament Research in convening an international meeting of experts at Geneva in August 1999 on developments in the field of information and telecommunications in the context of international security, as well as its results,

Considering that the assessments of the Member States contained in the reports of the Secretary-General and the international meeting of experts have contributed to a better understanding of the substance of issues of international information security and related notions,

1. *Calls upon* Member States to promote further at multilateral levels the consideration of existing and potential threats in the field of information security, as well as possible measures to limit the threats emerging in this field;

2. *Considers* that the purpose of such measures could be served through the examination of relevant international concepts aimed at strengthening the security of global information and telecommunications systems;

3. *Invites* all Member States to continue to inform the Secretary-General of their views and assessments on the following questions:

(*a*) General appreciation of the issues of information security;

(*b*) Definition of basic notions related to information security, including unauthorized interference with or misuse of information and telecommunications systems and information resources;

(*c*) The content of the concepts mentioned in paragraph 2 of the present resolution;

4. *Requests* the Secretary-General to submit a report based on replies received from Member States to the General Assembly at its fifty-sixth session;

5. *Decides* to include in the provisional agenda of its fifty-sixth session the item entitled "Developments in the field of information and telecommunications in the context of international security".

69th plenary meeting
20 November 2000

---

[2] A/54/213 and A/55/140 and Corr.1 and Add.1.

2

201

 **General Assembly**

Distr.: General
7 January 2002

Fifty-sixth session
Agenda item 69

Resolution adopted by the General Assembly

[on the report of the First Committee (A/56/533)]

**56/19.   Developments in the field of information and
telecommunications in the context of international
security**

The General Assembly,

Recalling its resolutions 53/70 of 4 December 1998, 54/49 of 1 December 1999 and 55/28 of 20 November 2000,

Recalling also its resolutions on the role of science and technology in the context of international security, in which, inter alia, it recognized that scientific and technological developments could have both civilian and military applications and that progress in science and technology for civilian applications needed to be maintained and encouraged,

Noting that considerable progress has been achieved in developing and applying the latest information technologies and means of telecommunication,

Affirming that it sees in this process the broadest positive opportunities for the further development of civilization, the expansion of opportunities for cooperation for the common good of all States, the enhancement of the creative potential of mankind and additional improvements in the circulation of information in the global community,

Recalling, in this connection, the approaches and principles outlined at the Information Society and Development Conference, held at Midrand, South Africa, from 13 to 15 May 1996,

Bearing in mind the results of the Ministerial Conference on Terrorism, held in Paris on 30 July 1996, and the recommendations that it made,[1]

Noting that the dissemination and use of information technologies and means affect the interests of the entire international community and that optimum effectiveness is enhanced by broad international cooperation,

Expressing concern that these technologies and means can potentially be used for purposes that are inconsistent with the objectives of maintaining international

---

[1] See A/51/261, annex.

01 47628

stability and security and may adversely affect the security of States in both civil and military fields,

Considering that it is necessary to prevent the use of information resources or technologies for criminal or terrorist purposes,

Noting the contribution of those Member States that have submitted their assessments on issues of information security to the Secretary-General pursuant to paragraphs 1 to 3 of resolutions 53/70, 54/49 and 55/28,

Taking note of the reports of the Secretary-General containing those assessments,[2]

Welcoming the initiative taken by the Secretariat and the United Nations Institute for Disarmament Research in convening an international meeting of experts at Geneva in August 1999 on developments in the field of information and telecommunications in the context of international security, as well as its results,

Considering that the assessments of the Member States contained in the reports of the Secretary-General and the international meeting of experts have contributed to a better understanding of the substance of issues of international information security and related notions,

1.   *Calls upon* Member States to promote further at multilateral levels the consideration of existing and potential threats in the field of information security, as well as possible measures to limit the threats emerging in this field, consistent with the need to preserve the free flow of information;

2.   *Considers* that the purpose of such measures could be served through the examination of relevant international concepts aimed at strengthening the security of global information and telecommunications systems;

3.   *Invites* all Member States to continue to inform the Secretary-General of their views and assessments on the following questions:

(*a*)   General appreciation of the issues of information security;

(*b*)   Definition of basic notions related to information security, including unauthorized interference with or misuse of information and telecommunications systems and information resources;

(*c*)   The content of the concepts mentioned in paragraph 2 of the present resolution;

4.   *Requests* the Secretary-General to consider existing and potential threats in the sphere of information security and possible cooperative measures to address them, and to conduct a study on the concepts referred to in paragraph 2 of the present resolution, with the assistance of a group of governmental experts, to be established in 2004, appointed by him on the basis of equitable geographical distribution and with the help of Member States in a position to render such assistance, and to submit a report on the outcome of the study to the General Assembly at its sixtieth session;

---

[2] A/54/213, A/55/140 and Corr.1 and Add.1, and A/56/164 and Add.1.

5.   *Decides* to include in the provisional agenda of its fifty-seventh session the item entitled "Developments in the field of information and telecommunications in the context of international security".

68th plenary meeting
29 November 2001

3

204

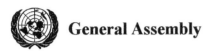 **General Assembly**

Distr.: General
30 December 2002

Fifty-seventh session
Agenda item 61

Resolution adopted by the General Assembly

[on the report of the First Committee (A/57/505)]

57/53. Developments in the field of information and telecommunications in the context of international security

The General Assembly,

Recalling its resolutions 53/70 of 4 December 1998, 54/49 of 1 December 1999, 55/28 of 20 November 2000 and 56/19 of 29 November 2001,

Recalling also its resolutions on the role of science and technology in the context of international security, in which, inter alia, it recognized that scientific and technological developments could have both civilian and military applications and that progress in science and technology for civilian applications needed to be maintained and encouraged,

Noting that considerable progress has been achieved in developing and applying the latest information technologies and means of telecommunication,

Affirming that it sees in this process the broadest positive opportunities for the further development of civilization, the expansion of opportunities for cooperation for the common good of all States, the enhancement of the creative potential of humankind and additional improvements in the circulation of information in the global community,

Recalling, in this connection, the approaches and principles outlined at the Information Society and Development Conference, held in Midrand, South Africa, from 13 to 15 May 1996,

Bearing in mind the results of the Ministerial Conference on Terrorism, held in Paris on 30 July 1996, and the recommendations that it made,[1]

Noting that the dissemination and use of information technologies and means affect the interests of the entire international community and that optimum effectiveness is enhanced by broad international cooperation,

Expressing concern that these technologies and means can potentially be used for purposes that are inconsistent with the objectives of maintaining international

---

[1] See A/51/261, annex.

02 54145

stability and security and may adversely affect the integrity of the infrastructure of States to the detriment of their security in both civil and military fields,

Considering that it is necessary to prevent the use of information resources or technologies for criminal or terrorist purposes,

Noting the contribution of those Member States that have submitted their assessments on issues of information security to the Secretary-General pursuant to paragraphs 1 to 3 of resolutions 53/70, 54/49, 55/28 and 56/19,

Taking note of the reports of the Secretary-General containing those assessments,[2]

Welcoming the initiative taken by the Secretariat and the United Nations Institute for Disarmament Research in convening an international meeting of experts in Geneva in August 1999 on developments in the field of information and telecommunications in the context of international security, as well as its results,

Considering that the assessments of the Member States contained in the reports of the Secretary-General and the international meeting of experts have contributed to a better understanding of the substance of issues of international information security and related notions,

Confirming the request to the Secretary-General contained in paragraph 4 of its resolution 56/19,

1. *Calls upon* Member States to promote further at multilateral levels the consideration of existing and potential threats in the field of information security, as well as possible measures to limit the threats emerging in this field, consistent with the need to preserve the free flow of information;

2. *Considers* that the purpose of such measures could be served through the examination of relevant international concepts aimed at strengthening the security of global information and telecommunications systems;

3. *Invites* all Member States to continue to inform the Secretary-General of their views and assessments on the following questions:

(*a*) General appreciation of the issues of information security;

(*b*) Definition of basic notions related to information security, including unauthorized interference with or misuse of information and telecommunications systems and information resources;

(*c*) The content of the concepts mentioned in paragraph 2 of the present resolution;

4. *Requests* the Secretary-General to consider existing and potential threats in the sphere of information security and possible cooperative measures to address them, and to conduct a study on the concepts referred to in paragraph 2 of the present resolution, with the assistance of a group of governmental experts, to be established in 2004, appointed by him on the basis of equitable geographical distribution and with the help of Member States in a position to render such assistance, and to submit a report on the outcome of the study to the General Assembly at its sixtieth session;

---

[2] A/54/213, A/55/140 and Corr.1 and Add.1, A/56/164 and Add.1 and A/57/166 and Add.1.

5. *Decides* to include in the provisional agenda of its fifty-eighth session the item entitled "Developments in the field of information and telecommunications in the context of international security".

57th plenary meeting
22 November 2002

3

 **General Assembly**

Distr.: General
18 December 2003

Fifty-eighth session
Agenda item 68

Resolution adopted by the General Assembly

[*on the report of the First Committee (A/58/457)*]

58/32.   Developments in the field of information and telecommunications in the context of international security

The General Assembly,

Recalling its resolutions 53/70 of 4 December 1998, 54/49 of 1 December 1999, 55/28 of 20 November 2000, 56/19 of 29 November 2001 and 57/53 of 22 November 2002,

Recalling also its resolutions on the role of science and technology in the context of international security, in which, inter alia, it recognized that scientific and technological developments could have both civilian and military applications and that progress in science and technology for civilian applications needed to be maintained and encouraged,

Noting that considerable progress has been achieved in developing and applying the latest information technologies and means of telecommunication,

Affirming that it sees in this process the broadest positive opportunities for the further development of civilization, the expansion of opportunities for cooperation for the common good of all States, the enhancement of the creative potential of humankind and additional improvements in the circulation of information in the global community,

Recalling, in this connection, the approaches and principles outlined at the Information Society and Development Conference, held in Midrand, South Africa, from 13 to 15 May 1996,

Bearing in mind the results of the Ministerial Conference on Terrorism, held in Paris on 30 July 1996, and the recommendations that it made,[1]

Noting that the dissemination and use of information technologies and means affect the interests of the entire international community and that optimum effectiveness is enhanced by broad international cooperation,

---

[1] See A/51/261, annex.

03 45483

Expressing its concern that these technologies and means can potentially be used for purposes that are inconsistent with the objectives of maintaining international stability and security and may adversely affect the integrity of the infrastructure of States to the detriment of their security in both civil and military fields,

Considering that it is necessary to prevent the use of information resources or technologies for criminal or terrorist purposes,

Noting the contribution of those Member States that have submitted their assessments on issues of information security to the Secretary-General pursuant to paragraphs 1 to 3 of resolutions 53/70, 54/49, 55/28, 56/19 and 57/53,

Taking note of the reports of the Secretary-General containing those assessments,[2]

Welcoming the initiative taken by the Secretariat and the United Nations Institute for Disarmament Research in convening an international meeting of experts in Geneva in August 1999 on developments in the field of information and telecommunications in the context of international security, as well as its results,

Considering that the assessments of the Member States contained in the reports of the Secretary-General and the international meeting of experts have contributed to a better understanding of the substance of issues of international information security and related notions,

Confirming the request to the Secretary-General contained in paragraph 4 of its resolutions 56/19 and 57/53,

1. *Calls upon* Member States to promote further at multilateral levels the consideration of existing and potential threats in the field of information security, as well as possible measures to limit the threats emerging in this field, consistent with the need to preserve the free flow of information;

2. *Considers* that the purpose of such measures could be served through the examination of relevant international concepts aimed at strengthening the security of global information and telecommunications systems;

3. *Invites* all Member States to continue to inform the Secretary-General of their views and assessments on the following questions:

    (*a*) General appreciation of the issues of information security;

    (*b*) Definition of basic notions related to information security, including unauthorized interference with or misuse of information and telecommunications systems and information resources;

    (*c*) The content of the concepts mentioned in paragraph 2 of the present resolution;

4. *Requests* the Secretary-General to consider existing and potential threats in the sphere of information security and possible cooperative measures to address them, and to conduct a study on the concepts referred to in paragraph 2 of the present resolution, with the assistance of a group of governmental experts, to be established in 2004, appointed by him on the basis of equitable geographical distribution and with the help of Member States in a position to render such

---

[2] A/54/213, A/55/140 and Corr.1 and Add.1, A/56/164 and Add.1, A/57/166 and Add.1 and A/58/373.

assistance, and to submit a report on the outcome of the study to the General Assembly at its sixtieth session;

5. *Decides* to include in the provisional agenda of its fifty-ninth session the item entitled "Developments in the field of information and telecommunications in the context of international security".

71st plenary meeting
8 December 2003

 **General Assembly**

Distr.: General
16 December 2004

Fifty-ninth session
Agenda item 60

Resolution adopted by the General Assembly

[on the report of the First Committee (A/59/454)]

59/61. Developments in the field of information and telecommunications in the context of international security

The General Assembly,

Recalling its resolutions 53/70 of 4 December 1998, 54/49 of 1 December 1999, 55/28 of 20 November 2000, 56/19 of 29 November 2001, 57/53 of 22 November 2002 and 58/32 of 8 December 2003,

Recalling also its resolutions on the role of science and technology in the context of international security, in which, inter alia, it recognized that scientific and technological developments could have both civilian and military applications and that progress in science and technology for civilian applications needed to be maintained and encouraged,

Noting that considerable progress has been achieved in developing and applying the latest information technologies and means of telecommunication,

Affirming that it sees in this process the broadest positive opportunities for the further development of civilization, the expansion of opportunities for cooperation for the common good of all States, the enhancement of the creative potential of humankind and additional improvements in the circulation of information in the global community,

Recalling, in this connection, the approaches and principles outlined at the Information Society and Development Conference, held in Midrand, South Africa, from 13 to 15 May 1996,

Bearing in mind the results of the Ministerial Conference on Terrorism, held in Paris on 30 July 1996, and the recommendations that it made,[1]

Noting that the dissemination and use of information technologies and means affect the interests of the entire international community and that optimum effectiveness is enhanced by broad international cooperation,

---

[1] See A/51/261, annex.

04-47992

Expressing its concern that these technologies and means can potentially be used for purposes that are inconsistent with the objectives of maintaining international stability and security and may adversely affect the integrity of the infrastructure of States to the detriment of their security in both civil and military fields,

Considering that it is necessary to prevent the use of information resources or technologies for criminal or terrorist purposes,

Noting the contribution of those Member States that have submitted their assessments on issues of information security to the Secretary-General pursuant to paragraphs 1 to 3 of resolutions 53/70, 54/49, 55/28, 56/19, 57/53 and 58/32,

Taking note of the reports of the Secretary-General containing those assessments,[2]

Welcoming the initiative taken by the Secretariat and the United Nations Institute for Disarmament Research in convening an international meeting of experts in Geneva in August 1999 on developments in the field of information and telecommunications in the context of international security, as well as its results,

Considering that the assessments of the Member States contained in the reports of the Secretary-General and the international meeting of experts have contributed to a better understanding of the substance of issues of international information security and related notions,

1. *Calls upon* Member States to promote further at multilateral levels the consideration of existing and potential threats in the field of information security, as well as possible measures to limit the threats emerging in this field, consistent with the need to preserve the free flow of information;

2. *Considers* that the purpose of such measures could be served through the examination of relevant international concepts aimed at strengthening the security of global information and telecommunications systems;

3. *Invites* all Member States to continue to inform the Secretary-General of their views and assessments on the following questions:

(*a*) General appreciation of the issues of information security;

(*b*) Definition of basic notions related to information security, including unauthorized interference with or misuse of information and telecommunications systems and information resources;

(*c*) The content of the concepts mentioned in paragraph 2 above;

4. *Notes with satisfaction* that the Secretary-General is considering existing and potential threats in the sphere of information security and possible cooperative measures to address them, and is conducting a study on the concepts referred to in paragraph 2 above, with the assistance of the group of governmental experts, established in 2004 pursuant to resolution 58/32, and will submit a report on the outcome of the study to the General Assembly at its sixtieth session;

5. *Also notes with satisfaction* that the group of governmental experts established by the Secretary-General held its first session from 12 to 16 July 2004 in

---

[2] A/54/213, A/55/140 and Corr.1 and Add.1, A/56/164 and Add.1, A/57/166 and Add.1, A/58/373 and A/59/116 and Add.1.

2

New York and that it intends to convene two more sessions in 2005 to fulfil its mandate specified in resolution 58/32;

6.   *Decides* to include in the provisional agenda of its sixtieth session the item entitled "Developments in the field of information and telecommunications in the context of international security".

66th plenary meeting
3 December 2004

3

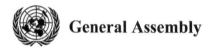

General Assembly

Distr.: General
6 January 2006

Sixtieth session
Agenda item 86

Resolution adopted by the General Assembly

[on the report of the First Committee (A/60/452)]

60/45. Developments in the field of information and telecommunications in the context of international security

The General Assembly,

Recalling its resolutions 53/70 of 4 December 1998, 54/49 of 1 December 1999, 55/28 of 20 November 2000, 56/19 of 29 November 2001, 57/53 of 22 November 2002, 58/32 of 8 December 2003, and 59/61 of 3 December 2004,

Recalling also its resolutions on the role of science and technology in the context of international security, in which, inter alia, it recognized that scientific and technological developments could have both civilian and military applications and that progress in science and technology for civilian applications needed to be maintained and encouraged,

Noting that considerable progress has been achieved in developing and applying the latest information technologies and means of telecommunication,

Affirming that it sees in this process the broadest positive opportunities for the further development of civilization, the expansion of opportunities for cooperation for the common good of all States, the enhancement of the creative potential of humankind and additional improvements in the circulation of information in the global community,

Recalling, in this connection, the approaches and principles outlined at the Information Society and Development Conference, held in Midrand, South Africa, from 13 to 15 May 1996,

Bearing in mind the results of the Ministerial Conference on Terrorism, held in Paris on 30 July 1996, and the recommendations that it made,[1]

Bearing in mind also the results of the first phase of the World Summit on the Information Society, held in Geneva from 10 to 12 December 2003,[2]

---

[1] See A/51/261, annex.
[2] See A/C.2/59/3.

05-49030

214

Noting that the dissemination and use of information technologies and means affect the interests of the entire international community and that optimum effectiveness is enhanced by broad international cooperation,

Expressing its concern that these technologies and means can potentially be used for purposes that are inconsistent with the objectives of maintaining international stability and security and may adversely affect the integrity of the infrastructure of States to the detriment of their security in both civil and military fields,

Considering that it is necessary to prevent the use of information resources or technologies for criminal or terrorist purposes,

Noting the contribution of those Member States that have submitted their assessments on issues of information security to the Secretary-General pursuant to paragraphs 1 to 3 of resolutions 53/70, 54/49, 55/28, 56/19, 57/53, 58/32 and 59/61,

Taking note of the reports of the Secretary-General containing those assessments,[3]

Welcoming the initiative taken by the Secretariat and the United Nations Institute for Disarmament Research in convening an international meeting of experts in Geneva in August 1999 on developments in the field of information and telecommunications in the context of international security, as well as its results,

Considering that the assessments of the Member States contained in the reports of the Secretary-General and the international meeting of experts have contributed to a better understanding of the substance of issues of international information security and related notions,

Bearing in mind that the Secretary-General, in fulfilment of resolution 58/32, established in 2004 a group of governmental experts, which, in accordance with its mandate, considered existing and potential threats in the sphere of information security and possible cooperative measures to address them and conducted a study on relevant international concepts aimed at strengthening the security of global information and telecommunications systems,

Taking note of the report of the Secretary-General on the Group of Governmental Experts on Developments in the Field of Information and Telecommunications in the Context of International Security, prepared on the basis of the results of the Group's work,[4]

1. *Calls upon* Member States to promote further at multilateral levels the consideration of existing and potential threats in the field of information security, as well as possible measures to limit the threats emerging in this field, consistent with the need to preserve the free flow of information;

2. *Considers* that the purpose of such measures could be served through the examination of relevant international concepts aimed at strengthening the security of global information and telecommunications systems;

3. *Invites* all Member States to continue to inform the Secretary-General of their views and assessments on the following questions:

---

[3] A/54/213, A/55/140 and Corr.1 and Add.1, A/56/164 and Add.1, A/57/166 and Add.1, A/58/373, A/59/116 and Add.1 and A/60/95 and Add.1.
[4] A/60/202.

(*a*)   General appreciation of the issues of information security;

(*b*)   Efforts taken at the national level to strengthen information security and promote international cooperation in this field;

(*c*)   The content of the concepts mentioned in paragraph 2 above;

(*d*)   Possible measures that could be taken by the international community to strengthen information security at the global level;

4.   *Requests* the Secretary-General, with the assistance of a group of governmental experts, to be established in 2009 on the basis of equitable geographical distribution, to continue to study existing and potential threats in the sphere of information security and possible cooperative measures to address them, as well as the concepts referred to in paragraph 2 above, and to submit a report on the results of this study to the General Assembly at its sixty-fifth session;

5.   *Decides* to include in the provisional agenda of its sixty-first session the item entitled "Developments in the field of information and telecommunications in the context of international security".

61st plenary meeting
8 December 2005

3

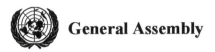 **General Assembly**

Distr.: General
19 December 2006

Sixty-first session
Agenda item 85

Resolution adopted by the General Assembly

[on the report of the First Committee (A/61/389)]

61/54. Developments in the field of information and telecommunications in the context of international security

The General Assembly,

Recalling its resolutions 53/70 of 4 December 1998, 54/49 of 1 December 1999, 55/28 of 20 November 2000, 56/19 of 29 November 2001, 57/53 of 22 November 2002, 58/32 of 8 December 2003, 59/61 of 3 December 2004 and 60/45 of 8 December 2005,

Recalling also its resolutions on the role of science and technology in the context of international security, in which, inter alia, it recognized that scientific and technological developments could have both civilian and military applications and that progress in science and technology for civilian applications needed to be maintained and encouraged,

Noting that considerable progress has been achieved in developing and applying the latest information technologies and means of telecommunication,

Affirming that it sees in this process the broadest positive opportunities for the further development of civilization, the expansion of opportunities for cooperation for the common good of all States, the enhancement of the creative potential of humankind and additional improvements in the circulation of information in the global community,

Recalling, in this connection, the approaches and principles outlined at the Information Society and Development Conference, held in Midrand, South Africa, from 13 to 15 May 1996,

Bearing in mind the results of the Ministerial Conference on Terrorism, held in Paris on 30 July 1996, and the recommendations that it made,[1]

Bearing in mind also the results of the World Summit on the Information Society, held in Geneva from 10 to 12 December 2003 (first phase) and in Tunis from 16 to 18 November 2005 (second phase),[2]

---

[1] See A/51/261, annex.
[2] See A/C.2/59/3 and A/60/687.

06-49767

Noting that the dissemination and use of information technologies and means affect the interests of the entire international community and that optimum effectiveness is enhanced by broad international cooperation,

Expressing its concern that these technologies and means can potentially be used for purposes that are inconsistent with the objectives of maintaining international stability and security and may adversely affect the integrity of the infrastructure of States to the detriment of their security in both civil and military fields,

Considering that it is necessary to prevent the use of information resources or technologies for criminal or terrorist purposes,

Noting the contribution of those Member States that have submitted their assessments on issues of information security to the Secretary-General pursuant to paragraphs 1 to 3 of resolutions 53/70, 54/49, 55/28, 56/19, 57/53, 58/32, 59/61 and 60/45,

Taking note of the reports of the Secretary-General containing those assessments,[3]

Welcoming the initiative taken by the Secretariat and the United Nations Institute for Disarmament Research in convening an international meeting of experts in Geneva in August 1999 on developments in the field of information and telecommunications in the context of international security, as well as its results,

Considering that the assessments of the Member States contained in the reports of the Secretary-General and the international meeting of experts have contributed to a better understanding of the substance of issues of international information security and related notions,

Bearing in mind that the Secretary-General, in fulfilment of resolution 58/32, established in 2004 a group of governmental experts, which, in accordance with its mandate, considered existing and potential threats in the sphere of information security and possible cooperative measures to address them and conducted a study on relevant international concepts aimed at strengthening the security of global information and telecommunications systems,

Taking note of the report of the Secretary-General on the Group of Governmental Experts on Developments in the Field of Information and Telecommunications in the Context of International Security, prepared on the basis of the results of the Group's work,[4]

1.　*Calls upon* Member States to promote further at multilateral levels the consideration of existing and potential threats in the field of information security, as well as possible measures to limit the threats emerging in this field, consistent with the need to preserve the free flow of information;

2.　*Considers* that the purpose of such measures could be served through the examination of relevant international concepts aimed at strengthening the security of global information and telecommunications systems;

---

[3] A/54/213, A/55/140 and Corr.1 and Add.1, A/56/164 and Add.1, A/57/166 and Add.1, A/58/373, A/59/116 and Add.1, A/60/95 and Add.1 and A/61/161.
[4] A/60/202.

2

3. *Invites* all Member States to continue to inform the Secretary-General of their views and assessments on the following questions:

(*a*)   General appreciation of the issues of information security;

(*b*)   Efforts taken at the national level to strengthen information security and promote international cooperation in this field;

(*c*)   The content of the concepts mentioned in paragraph 2 above;

(*d*)   Possible measures that could be taken by the international community to strengthen information security at the global level;

4. *Requests* the Secretary-General, with the assistance of a group of governmental experts, to be established in 2009 on the basis of equitable geographical distribution, to continue to study existing and potential threats in the sphere of information security and possible cooperative measures to address them, as well as the concepts referred to in paragraph 2 above, and to submit a report on the results of this study to the General Assembly at its sixty-fifth session;

5. *Decides* to include in the provisional agenda of its sixty-second session the item entitled "Developments in the field of information and telecommunications in the context of international security".

67th plenary meeting
6 December 2006

3

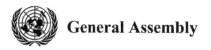

General Assembly

Distr.: General
8 January 2008

Sixty-second session
Agenda item 93

Resolution adopted by the General Assembly

[on the report of the First Committee (A/62/386)]

62/17. Developments in the field of information and telecommunications in the context of international security

The General Assembly,

Recalling its resolutions 53/70 of 4 December 1998, 54/49 of 1 December 1999, 55/28 of 20 November 2000, 56/19 of 29 November 2001, 57/53 of 22 November 2002, 58/32 of 8 December 2003, 59/61 of 3 December 2004, 60/45 of 8 December 2005 and 61/54 of 6 December 2006,

Recalling also its resolutions on the role of science and technology in the context of international security, in which, inter alia, it recognized that scientific and technological developments could have both civilian and military applications and that progress in science and technology for civilian applications needed to be maintained and encouraged,

Noting that considerable progress has been achieved in developing and applying the latest information technologies and means of telecommunication,

Affirming that it sees in this process the broadest positive opportunities for the further development of civilization, the expansion of opportunities for cooperation for the common good of all States, the enhancement of the creative potential of humankind and additional improvements in the circulation of information in the global community,

Recalling, in this connection, the approaches and principles outlined at the Information Society and Development Conference, held in Midrand, South Africa, from 13 to 15 May 1996,

Bearing in mind the results of the Ministerial Conference on Terrorism, held in Paris on 30 July 1996, and the recommendations that it made,[1]

Bearing in mind also the results of the World Summit on the Information Society, held in Geneva from 10 to 12 December 2003 (first phase) and in Tunis from 16 to 18 November 2005 (second phase),[2]

---

[1] See A/51/261, annex.
[2] See A/C.2/59/3 and A/60/687.

07-46479

Noting that the dissemination and use of information technologies and means affect the interests of the entire international community and that optimum effectiveness is enhanced by broad international cooperation,

Expressing its concern that these technologies and means can potentially be used for purposes that are inconsistent with the objectives of maintaining international stability and security and may adversely affect the integrity of the infrastructure of States to the detriment of their security in both civil and military fields,

Considering that it is necessary to prevent the use of information resources or technologies for criminal or terrorist purposes,

Noting the contribution of those Member States that have submitted their assessments on issues of information security to the Secretary-General pursuant to paragraphs 1 to 3 of resolutions 53/70, 54/49, 55/28, 56/19, 57/53, 58/32, 59/61, 60/45 and 61/54,

Taking note of the reports of the Secretary-General containing those assessments,[3]

Welcoming the initiative taken by the Secretariat and the United Nations Institute for Disarmament Research in convening an international meeting of experts in Geneva in August 1999 on developments in the field of information and telecommunications in the context of international security, as well as its results,

Considering that the assessments of the Member States contained in the reports of the Secretary-General and the international meeting of experts have contributed to a better understanding of the substance of issues of international information security and related notions,

Bearing in mind that the Secretary-General, in fulfilment of resolution 58/32, established in 2004 a group of governmental experts, which, in accordance with its mandate, considered existing and potential threats in the sphere of information security and possible cooperative measures to address them and conducted a study on relevant international concepts aimed at strengthening the security of global information and telecommunications systems,

Taking note of the report of the Secretary-General on the Group of Governmental Experts on Developments in the Field of Information and Telecommunications in the Context of International Security, prepared on the basis of the results of the Group's work,[4]

1. *Calls upon* Member States to promote further at multilateral levels the consideration of existing and potential threats in the field of information security, as well as possible measures to limit the threats emerging in this field, consistent with the need to preserve the free flow of information;

2. *Considers* that the purpose of such measures could be served through the examination of relevant international concepts aimed at strengthening the security of global information and telecommunications systems;

---

[3] A/54/213, A/55/140 and Corr.1 and Add.1, A/56/164 and Add.1, A/57/166 and Add.1, A/58/373, A/59/116 and Add.1, A/60/95 and Add.1, and A/61/161 and Add.1.

[4] A/60/202.

2

3.	*Invites* all Member States to continue to inform the Secretary-General of their views and assessments on the following questions:

(*a*)	General appreciation of the issues of information security;

(*b*)	Efforts taken at the national level to strengthen information security and promote international cooperation in this field;

(*c*)	The content of the concepts mentioned in paragraph 2 above;

(*d*)	Possible measures that could be taken by the international community to strengthen information security at the global level;

4.	*Requests* the Secretary-General, with the assistance of a group of governmental experts, to be established in 2009 on the basis of equitable geographical distribution, to continue to study existing and potential threats in the sphere of information security and possible cooperative measures to address them, as well as the concepts referred to in paragraph 2 above, and to submit a report on the results of this study to the General Assembly at its sixty-fifth session;

5.	*Decides* to include in the provisional agenda of its sixty-third session the item entitled "Developments in the field of information and telecommunications in the context of international security".

61st plenary meeting
5 December 2007

3

FINAL DETERMINATION
UNCLASSIFIED
L. M. Redman
JAN 23 '81

UNCLASSIFIED

20 April 1944

Subject: Possible Use of Radioactive Poison in Rocket Propelled, Unmanned Aircraft.

MEMORANDUM to Major General L. R. Groves.

1. During my last visit to Washington on 14 March 1944, I was accompanied by Major Furman to the Pentagon and there shown the present information on rocket installations and additional unknown construction on the sector in France between 100 and 150 miles from London and Bristol. It appeared that fairly definite information is available on the launching stations but very little is available on the seven to ten larger stations, and these are guarded with great energy.

2. At the time I could form no opinion as to the possible nature of the contemplated material except that it must be a very "hot" chemical since the installations were literally under the guns and bombs of the enemy, the opposite place where a delicate chemical job should be performed. from that in which.

3. Recently, I have discussed with Blotblats, one of Chadwick's men, the work done by Chadwick's group in England in connection with investigating the possibilities of radioactive poisons evolved from disintegration products of a pile. I understand that such a pile would not be extremely difficult to set up and operate and that it could be "milked" every three days. It would then be necessary to separate the radioactive materials and transport these behind very heavy lead armor to the launching point.

4. The combination of an apparent plan to use unmanned aircraft and the possibility that some form of complicated installation is being built in locations which might serve as feeders to the launching point, suggests the possibility that the "hot chemical" might be radioactive disintegration products which the Germans considered so "hot" that they could not transport them from manufacturing points in Germany by any available transportation. These might be placed in bombs with ordinary explosives to be functioning over the ground to gain maximum distribution of the radioactive products. It is unnecessary to picture the destructive possibilities of such an arrangement.

CLASSIFICATION CANCELLED
PER DOC REVIEW JAN. 1973
OK J.E.W. 4/17/74

UNCLASSIFIED

224

 UNCLASSIFIED

b. Essentials in the construction of a scheme such as outlined above would be:

　　a. Some material for lining a pile. This might be heavy water or blocks of graphite. Other possibilities exist.

　　b. Uranium for use in the pile. This might be in some liquid solution.

　　c. Heavy walls surrounding pile. It might be located in the ground.

　　d. A small chemical plant for separating the radioactive products. This would require heavy lead for protection of personnel.

　　e. During actual operation or rehearsal operation, blood counts would probably be taken of operating personnel.

　　f. Final loading and launching positions would probably be done behind heavy lead or very thick concrete protection.

　　　　　　　　　　　　　　　W. S. PARSONS,
　　　　　　　　　　　　　　　Captain, U.S.N.

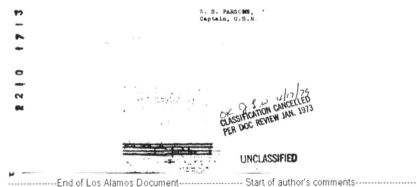

UNCLASSIFIED

---------------End of Los Alamos Document--------------------- Start of author's comments--------------------

The intention to use the latest vehicle to launch a biochemical attack is traceable. This document illustrates how far forward-thinking took certain scientists and intelligence officers (since the late 1930's) in their respective roles as engineers and investigators [to come up with scientific breakthroughs and anticipate (uncover) the most dreadful threats].

TOMORROW'S POSSIBLY DEADLIEST DIFFUSERS OF BIOACTIVE SUBSTANCES

---- Release starts here----

LOCKHEED MARTIN TO DESIGN NANO AIR VEHICLE TO MONITOR THE URBAN BATTLEFIELD

PRESS RELEASE OF JULY, 20, 2006

[According to Lockheed's Stephen P. O'Neill]

BATTLEFIELDCHERRY HILL, NJ, July 20, 2006—The Defense Advanced Research Projects Agency(DARPA) awarded Lockheed Martin (NYSE:LMT) a $1.7-million, 10-month contract to design a revolutionary remote-controlled nano air vehicle (NAV) that will collect military intelligence indoors and outdoors on the urban battlefield.

Lockheed Martin Advanced Technology Laboratories (ATL) leads a team that will design a remote-controlled NAV, similar in size and shape to a maple tree seed. A chemical rocket enclosed in its one-bladed wing will power a sensor payload module more than 1,100 yards. Delivered from a hover and weighing up to 0.07 ounces, the module will be interchangeable based on mission requirements. Besides controlling lift and pitch, the wing will also house telemetry, communications, navigation, imaging sensors, and battery power. The NAV will be about 1.5 inches long and have a maximum takeoff weight of about 0.35 ounces.

In typical operation, a war fighter will launch the NAV and fly it toward the target by viewing its flight path through a camera embedded in the wing. Like a maple tree seed, the one-bladed device will rotate in flight, but its camera will provide a stable forward view and transmit images back to a small, hand-held display. As the system matures, a simple autopilot aboard the NAV will provide limited autonomous operations. Once the NAV delivers its payload, it will return to the war fighter for collection and refurbishment.

According to James Marsh, ATL director, designing and building such a small device will require revolutionary manufacturing technologies to integrate near-microscopic components into the airframe. But even the airframe will require a challenging combination of new and emerging technologies.

"The challenges are both exciting and daunting, because some of the technologies vital to our success have yet to be discovered," Marsh said. "We know going in that we need some of the best minds in manufacturing technology and in the development and integration of highly sophisticated, software-driven, control technologies and mission systems."

The contract will fund conceptual design and risk reduction using prototypes of the engine, airframe, flight control system, and communications system as well as computer models of the guidance system and sensors. Following a successful preliminary design review planned for summer 2007 and a sequence of go/no-go tests, DARPA may fund an additional 18-monthperiod during which Lockheed Martin will design and test a flying prototype.

Lockheed Martin ATL leads a team that includes Lockheed Martin Advanced Development Programs (Skunk Works), Lockheed Martin Advanced Technology Center, the Lockheed Martin-managed Sandia National Laboratories, AeroCraft, ATK Thiokol and the University of Pennsylvania.

Lockheed Martin's NAV program is part of a DARPA effort from its Defense Sciences Office to improve the quality, quantity, and reliability of information gathered and transmitted by unattended ground sensors. The effectiveness of these sensors may be dependent on their precise location. Achieving optimal monitoring and communication often requires precise deployment of sensors.

####

----Release ends here----

US 20070020153A1

(19) **United States**

(12) **Patent Application Publication** (10) Pub. No.: **US 2007/0020153 A1**
Hyacinthe   (43) Pub. Date: **Jan. 25, 2007**

(54) SYSTEM AND DEVICE FOR PREVENTION
AND NEUTRALIZATION OF BIOACTIVE
SUBSTANCES AND GENERATING AN
AROMA-PRODUCING SUBSTANCE

(76) Inventor: **Berg P. Hyacinthe**, Tallahassee, FL
(US)

Correspondence Address:
DENNIS L. COOK, ESQ.
THE LAW OFFICES OF DENNIS L COOK
PLLC
12718 DUPONT CIRCLE
TAMPA, FL 33626 (US)

(21) Appl. No.:   **11/330,875**

(22) Filed: **Jan. 12, 2006**

Related U.S. Application Data

(60) Provisional application No. 60/700,708, filed on Jul.
19, 2005.

Publication Classification

(51) Int. Cl.
A61L 9/12   (2007.01)
(52) U.S. Cl. **422/124**; 422/306

(57)   **ABSTRACT**

An on-demand system for preventing and/neutralizing bioactive substances employs real time monitoring of the fluid
for bioactive substances. Once a specific bioactive substance
is detected, then a specific neutralizing substance is selected,
such as an oxidizing substance, intense ultraviolet light, a
neutralizing substance or other substances selected for particular threats. In another example of the invention, a device
neutralizing a substance would include a container that
would be capable of containing each of the plurality of
precursors, a collecting space for receiving each of the
plurality of precursors selected by the selector, and a dispensing mechanism for dispensing the neutralizing substance. In one example the neutralizing substance is formu-
lated by the reactions of the precursors in order to neutralize
the substance. The device may alternatively select a plurality
of precursors to produce an aroma-producing substance and
alternatively may neutralize the aroma-producing substance
if it harmful or lethal, for example.

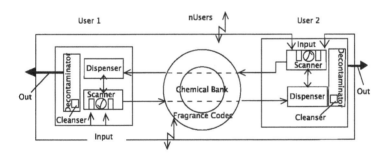

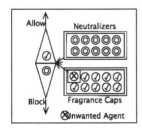

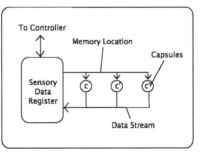

229

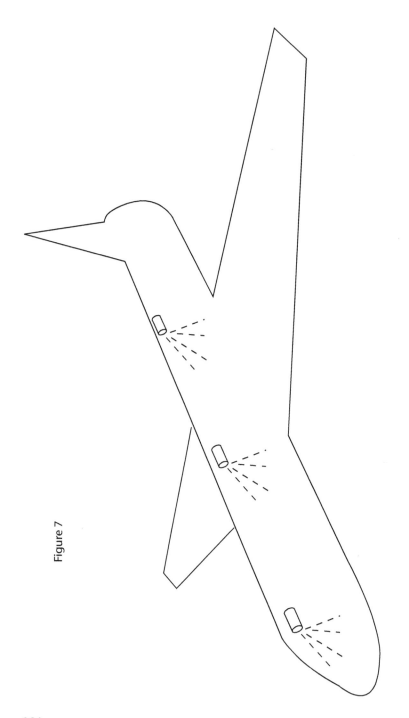

Figure 7

(19) **United States**

(12) **Patent Application Publication** (10) Pub. No.: **US 2006/0199614 A1**

Hyacinthe (43) **Pub. Date:** **Sep. 7, 2006**

(54) **UNIVERSAL CELLULAR CIRCUIT BOARD**

(76) Inventor: **Berg P. Hyacinthe**, Tallahassee, FL (US)

Correspondence Address:
DENNIS L. COOK, ESQ.
THE LAW OFFICES OF DENNIS L COOK
PLLC
12718 DUPONT CIRCLE
TAMPA, FL 33626 (US)

(21) Appl. No.: **11/271,715**

(22) Filed: **Nov. 12, 2005**

Related U.S. Application Data

(60) Provisional application No. 60/658,035, filed on Mar. 2, 2005.

Publication Classification

(51) **Int. Cl.**
H04B 1/38 (2006.01)

(52) U.S. Cl. **455/558**

(57) **ABSTRACT**

A system and apparatus that allows cell phone users to control the roaming features of their service from one telecommunication network (i.e., cellular service provider) to another at the device level, independently of a particular primary network. More specifically, it intends to perform primary functions using the principles of (SoC) design, allowing an array of third party smart cards to share the motherboard of the universal cellular circuit, thus, allowing for ease of switching service providers by simply pushing a button on the apparatus. In addition, this device is equipped with a digital security diagnostic port (DSDP), allowing the scanning of the physical layer of the cellular circuit for unwanted/unexpected chips and other digital security breaches. For the cause of unprecedented efforts to accelerate the design, production, implementation, and distribution of new technologies (SoC design, ESL design, Robotics . . .), this invention addresses a future threat to human-computer interactions (HCI) and public safety.

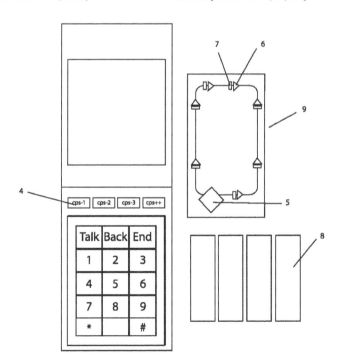

231

(19) **United States**

(12) **Patent Application Publication** (10) Pub. No.: US 2006/0124023 A1
Hyacinthe (43) Pub. Date: **Jun. 15, 2006**

(54) **EMERGENCY RESCUE VEHICLE**

(76) Inventor: **Berg P. Hyacinthe**, Tallahassee, FL
(US)

Correspondence Address:
**DENNIS L. COOK, ESQ.
THE LAW OFFICES OF DENNIS L COOK
PLLC
12718 DUPONT CIRCLE
TAMPA, FL 33626 (US)**

(21) Appl. No.: **11/296,608**

(22) Filed: **Dec. 7, 2005**

Related U.S. Application Data

(60) Provisional application No. 60/634,637, filed on Dec. 10, 2004.

Publication Classification

(51) **Int. Cl.**
B61B 15/00 (2006.01)
(52) **U.S. Cl.** 104/127

(57) **ABSTRACT**

The present invention relates to a rescue assembly including a vehicle that rides upon a track operated by a network of pistons set in a left to right array and connected by slanted bridges for control of said capsule. The vehicle, track, and piston network is all contained within a tube and is continuous vertically the entire height of a tall building or structure. The capsule is powered by an independent power source with regards to the building's or structure's power supply and is controlled via straight aerodynamic controls.

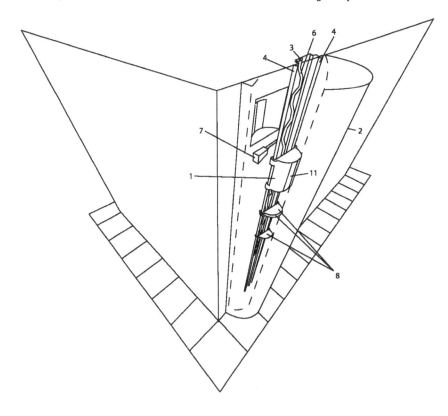

APPLYING THE EMERGENCY RESCUE VEHICLE IN
TIMELY RECOVERY OF FLIGHT DATA RECORDERS

As recent aircraft catastrophes have shown, the world's leading aircraft manufacturers are still struggling to find effective means of detecting special signals normally emitted by the telecommunication components of existing flight-data recording systems, following a disaster. The challenge is accentuated when flight-data recorders are buried under the ocean, hidden in deep ravines, lost in vast forests, or trapped atop of snowy mountains. Other factors, including limited battery life of electronic components, contribute to on-going efforts by the scientific community to find ways and develop technologies allowing for timely recovery of flight data and cockpit voice recorders (FDR/CVR). It is widely known that some spacecrafts have been equipped with remote flight data recovery systems. However, with a growing number of nations reaching for space capabilities, safety and security of communications satellites are threatened. For instance, direct-ascent ASAT missile systems constitute a growing threat in this arena. Moreover, 21st century "cyber warriors" are sharpening advanced interplanetary skills that will allow for the interception of protected communications channels anytime, anywhere. In short, satellite-based data recovery systems should be scrutinized before widespread adoption, for the threat intensifies with each technological innovation.

Other recovery systems involving mid-air ejection have been conceived, but failed to satisfy aircraft manufacturers and other stakeholders. In many cases, proposed legislations fail to "impose" widespread installation of "portable" backup FDR/CVR systems.

The proposed application features:

- An olfactive (natural/synthetic) signal system using a coated bioactive substance to release on-demand odors;
- A plurality of ultra-thin solar palettes;
- A circular ejectable capsule containing a plurality of parachutes intended to keep the FDR/CVR system afloat.
- Two mini pumps;
- A detachable data line linking backup system with main system (e.g., FDR/CVR);
- A floating storage compartment containing the backup FDR/CVR system;

- A custom security system to protect industrial secrets against unauthorized access (e.g., magnetic strips, real-time monitoring, and encryption);

- A tourniquet allowing synchronized deployment of parachutes and aiding against entanglement of parachute cables;

- A set of parachutes coated with a luminescent material, functioning as a "reflector" to be reasonably visible under severe weather conditions;

- An optional robotics component to serve as a mini "flight" stabilizer.

In summary, the floating "Wing-Tail" emergency rescue (WiTa) is proposed as an innovative means of securing timely recovery of (FDR/CVR) components following a catastrophe. It displays a new apparatus, an impact-triggered floatable device, a uniquely designed inflatable casing, an innovative gliding system, and a natural, energy-independent backup signal system.

P.S. This last concept is not available through the U.S. Patent and Trade Office.

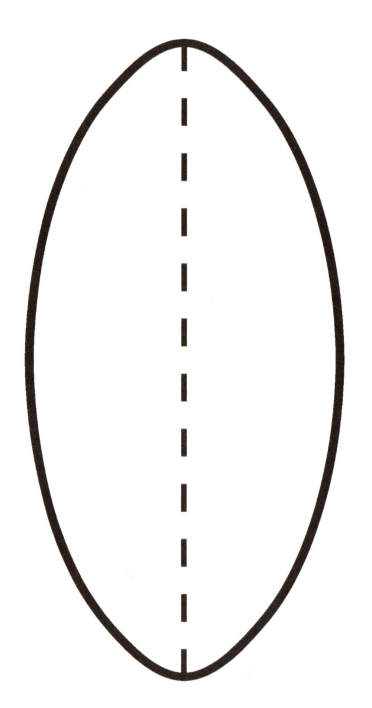

Figure 1. Bi-level Circular Embodiment

236

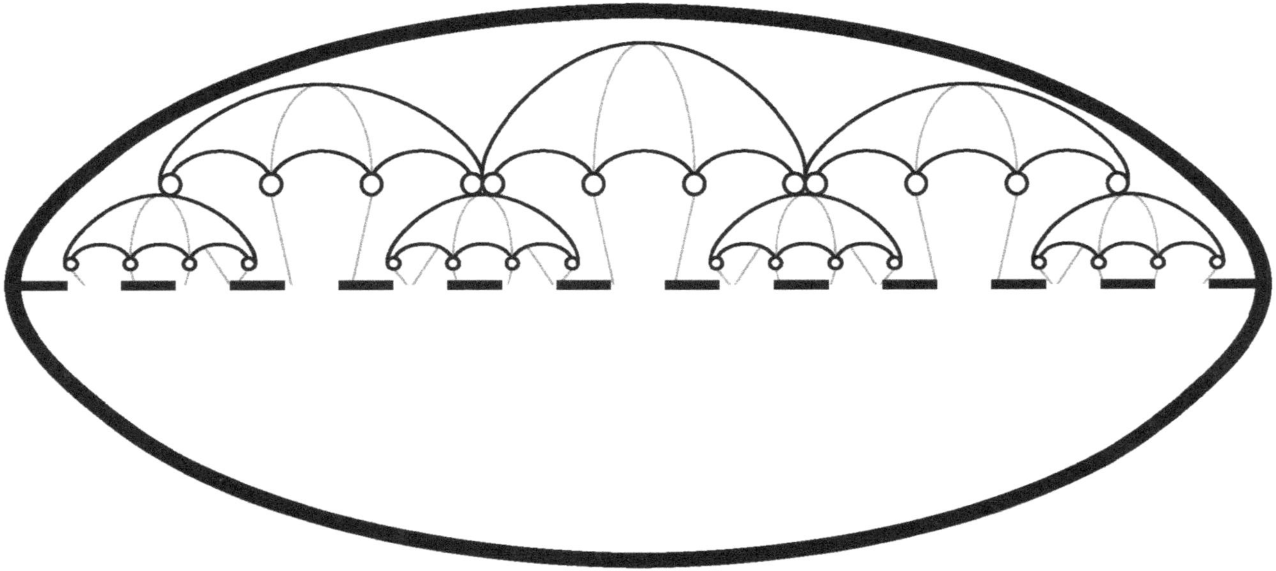

Figure 2. Initial Position of Folded Parachutes

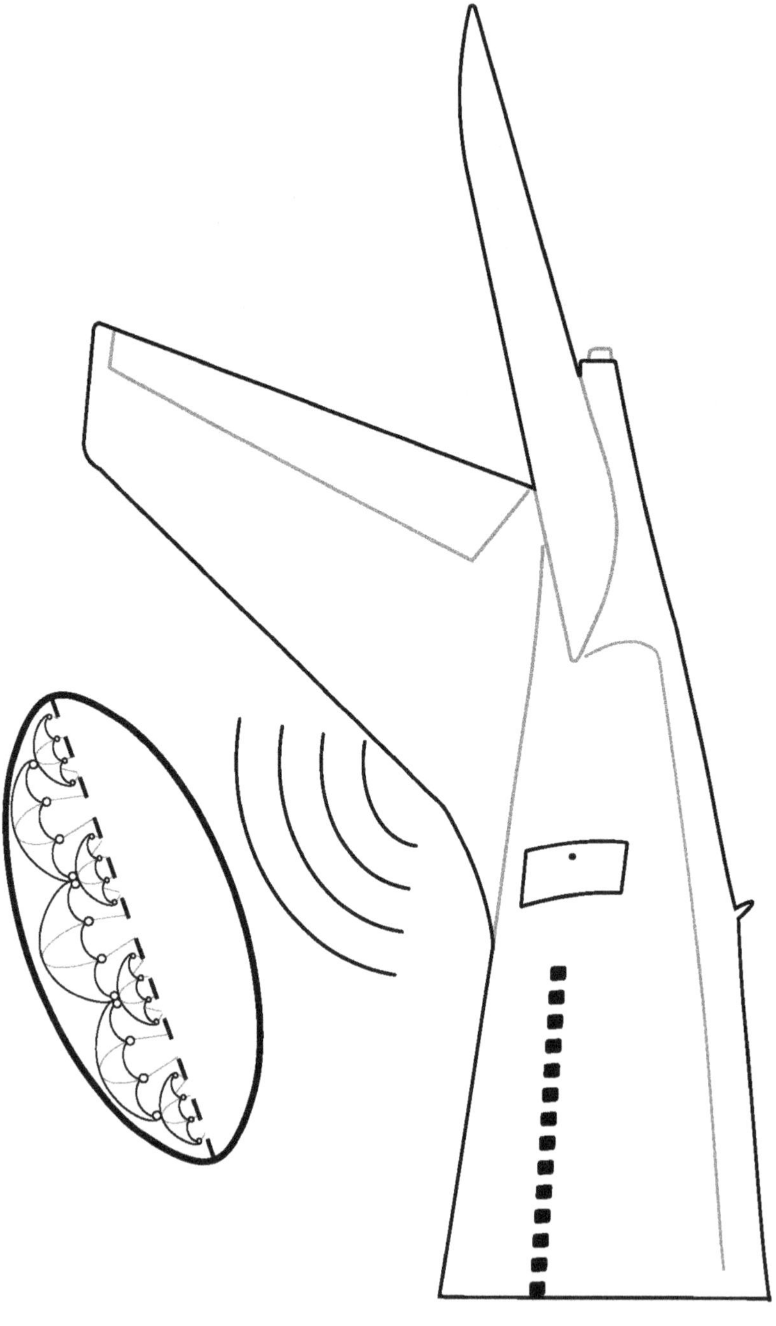

Figure 3. Release of Loaded Circular Shell

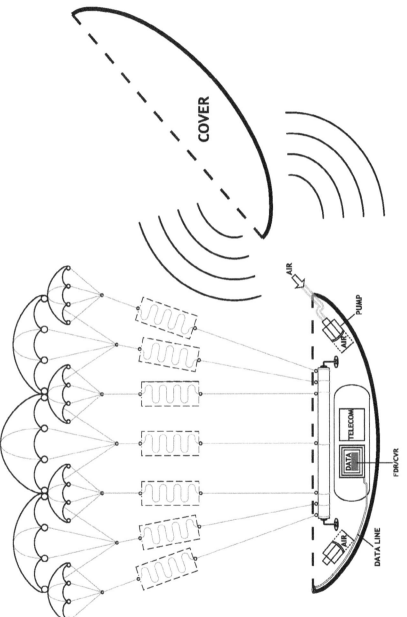

Figure 4. Post-deployment Phase of WiTa

www.ingramcontent.com/pod-product-compliance
Lightning Source LLC
Chambersburg PA
CBHW051231050326
40689CB00007B/884